INSIGHT INTO
36 STRATAGEMS

Editor In Chief: Ming Yan

Editor: Zi Wei, Xiao Ning, Li Shifen

Illustrator: Alina Yang

Proofreader: Li Shuang

ApphexBooks

TABLE OF CONTENTS

PREFACE

The 36 Stratagems is a unique collection of ancient Chinese proverbs commented as military tactics. Written in the Ming and Qing dynasties, its ideas originated from the famous military strategist Sun Wu in the Eastern Zhou period and the notable general Tan Daoji of the Southern and Northern dynasties. As an adjunct to Sun Tzu's The Art of War, the 36 stratagems illustrate a series of the most cunning and subtle tactics used in war and in politics, as well as in civilian life.

The stratagems are broken down into 6 categories, for the situations in which they are best used.

1 Winning Stratagems

The winning stratagems include: Cross the sea under camouflage; Besiege Wei to rescue Zhao; Kill with a borrowed knife; Wait at leisure while the enemy labors; Loot a burning house; Clamor in the east, then strike in the west. These stratagems mainly refer to taking actions in circumstances where your rival is stronger than you. The prerequisite is to have feasible plans in hand and favorable conditions on your side in order to defeat your rival and obtain greater benefits through the use of strategies.

2 Enemy Dealing Stratagems

The enemy dealing stratagems include: Create something from nothing; Sneak through the passage of Chencang; Observe the fire from the opposite shore; Hide your dagger behind a smile; Sacrifice plums to preserve peaches; Take the opportunity to pilfer a goat. These stratagems are mainly applied in tackling face-to-face conflicts between two sides. The victory in battle not only depends on the comparison of might and morale of two sides, but also relies on how you use the strategies and grasp the chances to weaken the enemy's combat capabilities in battle.

3 Attacking Stratagems

The attacking stratagems include: Stomp the grass to startle the snake; Borrow a corpse to resurrect the soul; Lure the tiger off its den; One must let loose in order to capture; Toss out a brick to obtain the jade; To defeat the bandits, capture their leader. These stratagems feature a stress on "use various means to crush the enemy's will of resistance at a small cost", pursuant to Sun Tzu's military thought in his essay "The Art of War", i.e. "the highest form of generalship is to thwart the enemy's plans; the next to the best is to prevent the junction of the enemy's forces; the inferior is to attack the enemy's army in the battlefield; and the worst one is to besiege and conquer walled cities."

4 Chaos Stratagems

The chaos stratagems include: Remove the firewood from under the pot; Stir up the water to catch fish; Slough off the cicada's golden shell; Shut the door to catch the thief; Befriend a distant state while attacking a neighbor; Obtain safe passage to conquer the Guo state. The core of these stratagems is to take full advantage of chaotic situations to obtain great benefits. In practical application, do something strange, unusual, and unexpected, leaving the opponent confused, and then tempting him to act on the wrong way so as to satisfy your intention.

5 Proximate Stratagems

The proximate stratagems include: Replace beams with rotten timbers; Point at mulberries while cursing locusts; Feign madness without becoming insane; Lure them onto the roof, then take away the ladder; Deck the tree with artificial blossoms; Turn from the guest into the host. These stratagems can be used in circumstances where both sides are evenly matched and locked in a stalemate, i.e. none of them has the possibility to catch fish and win in troubled waters and chaos, and the best policy is to adopt a favorable offensive and defensive tactic.

6 Desperate Stratagems

The desperate stratagems include: The beauty trap; The empty fort ruse; Counter-espionage; Self-torture ruse; Chain ruse; Retreat if all else fails. These stratagems can be applied to situations where your side is in danger, and the enemy is powerful and well-deployed, you have to draw up plans and carry out approaches to protect yourself; or you have already been defeated in search of revival and revenge.

This unique edition "Insight Into 36 Stratagems" supplies a clear and profound interpretation of the 36 related proverbs and illustrates them with cases not only from the battle scenarios in Chinese history and folklore but also from contemporary business and workplace affairs. In these cases, readers will enjoy the pragmatic tactics and brilliant thoughts that span time and space.

Whether you choose to fight, flee, deceive, or revel in the achievements of your business or career for the coming years, may the scales fall from your eyes, and may you learn from this handy, realistic handbook, in order to win in the end.

As the editor-in-chief of this edition, I would like to take this opportunity to express my heartfelt thanks to all the hard-working editors. Despite good intentions and conscientious efforts to avoid mistakes, it is likely to include at least some minor inaccuracies herein. I sincerely invite experts and fans of interest to give us their opinions and corrections, and readers are also welcome to leave valuable comments or feedback in the course of use.

Ming Yan

October 2020

Stratagem 1 · Cross the Sea Under Camouflage

Sun Tzu said: Mask your real goals, by using the ruse of a fake goal, until the real goal is achieved. Tactically, this is known as an 'open feint': publicly you point west when your goal is actually in the east.

This stratagem means that you mask your real goals, thus deceiving even the emperor (heaven) with a fake goal, until he is confronted with accomplished facts. Essentially, it makes use of the weaknesses of human nature that, people eventually become unaware of common daily activities, or events that keep repeating themselves, etc. When these happen, it is the best moment to carry out one's hidden real objective.

Emperor Tang Subdued Goguryeo

In 643 AD, Emperor Taizong of Tang baulked from crossing the sea to a campaign against Goguryeo. General Xue Rengui came up with a ruse to allay his fear of seasickness while crossing the sea. On a clear day, Taizong was invited to meet a wise man. They entered through a dark tunnel into a hall where they feasted. After feasting several days, Taizong heard the sound of waves and realized that he had been lured onto a ship! General Xue drew

7

aside the curtains to reveal the ocean and confessed that they had already crossed the sea. Upon discovering this, Taizong decided to carry on and won the campaign thereafter.

Double-Edged Sword: Business Negotiation

This stratagem is not only used in battlefields but also widely applied in marketplaces, workplaces, or even love affairs. For instance, doctors would say white lies to his incurable patients; old men may deceive girls with fancy words; Japan raided on Pearl Harbor during World War II with the trick of "cross the sea under camouflage". It can be used not only to protect the legitimate rights and interests of oneself and others, but also perhaps to seek improper benefits. Therefore, it is a "double-edged sword". In the workplace, this stratagem is commonly deployed for business negotiations and career advancements.

1) Business Negotiation

(1) Show your strength. When engaging in negotiations with a party, do not show your own will directly, just give an illusion of dissatisfaction or disapproval, and show them your alternative solutions. By this way, you can force the party to lower their demands and product pricing, or make certain concessions.

(2) Show your weakness. When many longing competitors are in the scene, humble yourself and exhibit the attitude of striving to visit and learn experience merely, show your weakness to paralyze them. Privately seize the time, revamp your plan, strengthen communications to enhance self-competitiveness.

The salespersons of Company A were discussing with the purchasing manager in the office. Company A requested to maintain the original asking price, but the purchasing manager believed that the current market was down and thereby the purchase price should go down a bit correspondingly.

While arguing, the secretary of the purchasing manager came in. She handed in a document to the manager and whispered: here's the facsimile from company B. Upon hearing of this, Company A immediately agreed to the request for the lower price being afraid its opponent Company B would snatch the customer away. In fact, there was no fax from Company B at all, it was just a trick of "crossing the sea under camouflage".

2) Career Advancement

In today's competitive society, people may "cross the sea under camouflage" either intentionally or unintentionally. Michael worked at a small company and wanted to move to a large one. He worked hard during the day while studied interview materials at night. All preparations were carried out in secret. Imagine if he had publicized his plan a lot, what would his colleagues and leaders have thought about this during the long periods before leaving?

Like battlefields, marketplaces and workplaces are full of intrigue. History sparkles with amusing examples of famous bureaucrats being taken down by those who seemed to be much close to them.

Sophia and Rose were good friends and colleagues. Once, there was a team leader position available in the department, and the manager needed to appoint either Sophia or Rose to serve. Knowing that they suddenly became competitors, both committed themselves to compete fairly without hurting their friendship. While Sophia worked hard and prepared for the competition, Rose actively recommended herself to the manager, saying that Sophia was inappropriate as she was currently in love, would be distracted, unable to work overtime, and later on would get married and have children, etc. Rose also added that, by contrast, she had no relevant planning within five years. In the end, the manager agreed with Rose's suggestion and appointed her as the team leader.

Stratagem 2 · Besiege Wei to Rescue Zhao

Sun Tzu said: When the enemy is too strong to be attacked directly, attack something they cherish. The idea is to avoid a head-on battle with a strong enemy, and instead strike at their weakness elsewhere. This will force the strong enemy to retreat in order to support their weakness. Battling against a tired and dispirited enemy will give a much higher chance of success.

Appear Where Unexpected

This proverb originated from the Warring States period. In 354 BC, the Wei state launched a battle against the Zhao state and besieged its capital Handan. Zhao turned to Qi for help, but the Qi general Sun Bin determined it would be unwise to confront strong Wei head-on, so he attacked its capital Daliang instead. When the Wei general Pang Juan heard that his capital was being attacked， he rushed back his army to defend the capital. In the haste of withdrawal, the tired troops of Wei were ambushed and defeated at the Battle of Guiling. Zhao was thus rescued while Pang barely escaped back to Wei to recoup his losses.

A Circuitous Route to Sales

The stratagem is also commonly used for various business activities such as marketing and sales, task delegation, personal promotion and career advancement. The key is how to opt for detours or back-up measures to tackle the problems incurred.

1) Take a Circuitous Route to Increase Sales

Salesperson Benjamin of company A complained that although his company produces goods and services better than its rivals, the product pricing is also higher. It seemed that the purchasing manager of company B had been brainwashed by the rivals — no matter how hard they persuaded, still he was looking for the goods and services from the rivals.

The sales manager said in reply: Since we can't get the purchasing department, why not try the technical department?

In the end, Benjamin settled the technical department. At the project level, the technical department raised the technical threshold of the product (to better serve customers and meet their needs). Therefore, the purchasing department had to purchase better goods/services from company A.

In the workplace, as it is said, the outcome is the goal, but there are many ways to attain the ultimate goal, so you don't have to directly focus on it. Opting for detours can help you achieve success in some circumstances.

2) Task Delegation

Benjamin was a salesperson at a small company, he usually worked flat out on multiple tasks simultaneously. One day around 4:30pm, as usual, he made himself a cup of coffee, prepared to submit his daily report through the web portal, then he could knock off at 5pm and attend a friend's party. At this moment, his manager suddenly came over and assigned him an urgent task that is needed to be done by 6pm.

When Benjamin put aside the things in hand and started to work on the urgent task, he got a phone call from the vice president who asked him if he could join an instant meeting with a vip customer. Knowing that the meeting would last for over one hour, Benjamin didn't refuse directly but handed over the phone to his manager, letting the superiors communicate with each other and determine which one (the urgent task or instant meeting) was in a higher priority.

If Benjamin directly refused to join the meeting, that would be somewhat offensive. In this case, it is better to leave the problem to superiors to deal with by themselves. Keep in mind, don't display negative feelings towards multi-tasking or having a heavy workload, be sure to organize and prioritize your tasks, aim to tackle the more difficult parts of a project early on in a day — if you wait until the end of a day to tackle the tough parts, you stand the chance of running out of time.

3) Personal Promotion

Sophia and Rose joined the sales department at the same time. The general manager Peter decided to appoint one person as the deputy manager. Regarding the ability, he would choose either Sophia or Rose from the department. Upon knowing of that, Sophia deliberately showed weakness and praised Rose everywhere. Rose was dead chuffed and seemed complacent at the office.

Sophia then made a rumour in secret about their colleague Grace, saying that although Grace was not very capable, she still wanted to get the deputy position because she had been very close to Peter recently. Rose believed the rumour and gradually singled Grace out, and eventually dissed each other.

Through the use of "besiege Wei to rescue Zhao", Sophia was playing "fisherman" who benefits when a snipe and clam quarrel. Note that this example is merely for the illustration of the stratagem here, it is not advocating anyone to be Sophia, but at least not to be Rose passively. In the workplace, when your opponent is strong, or when it is hard to predict the outcome, it is better to transfer the target appropriately and weaken the opponent through a series of operations enhancing your competitiveness.

Stratagem 3 · Kill with a Borrowed Knife

 3. 借刀杀人

Sun Tzu said: When you do not have the means to attack your enemy directly, then use the strength of another. For instance, trick an ally into attacking them, bribe their officials to turn traitor, or use the enemy's own strength against them.

Those who kill someone with a borrowed knife don't need to go shirtless, or consume their own strength, or even incur criminal liability. Throughout the ages, not only insidious villains tend to kill their rivals with borrowed knives, even magnanimous gentlemen, under certain circumstances, may deploy the ruse. Thereby, for a gentleman, even if unwilling to use it, he must learn to see through and guard against it without being used as a knife for some reason.

This ruse is also widely applied in the business arena. Its main purpose is to borrow human, material and financial resources to achieve one's goals. Seasoned negotiators are capable of making use of all available opportunities/conditions and borrowing social forces (public opinion, etc.) to put pressure on the other party; or using legal provisions and regulations to refute the other party's unreasonable demands in order to safeguard their own legitimate interests.

Killing Three Warriors with Two Peaches

During the Spring and Autumn period, Duke Jing of Qi had three generals, Gongsun Jie, Tian Kaijiang and Gu Yezi, in his employ. While the three were all capable and fearless warriors, their arrogance towards other ministers convinced Yan Ying, the prime minister of Qi, that they would have to be removed.

He therefore devised a ruse where two peaches were presented, purportedly as a reward, to the three generals; the two with the greatest accomplishment would get a peach each. Gongsun and Tian thought they deserved and took one peach each, while Gu angrily pulled his sword and challenged them to fight a duel. At last Gongsun and Tian felt ashamed of arguing fiercely just for two peaches and then committed suicide with their swords. Gu, shamed at having killed two colleagues by his boasting, then killed himself too. Thus Yan was able to remove three potential threats to the stability of Qi without breaking a sweat.

The Dark Wisdom Behind the Oriole

There is no lack of interest entanglements everywhere, strifes and conflicts behind the entanglements, no matter whether they are open or not, are extremely cruel indeed. You have no chance to choose a pure land: either succeed or fail to withdraw. Therefore, in the workplace, learning to guard the benefits you deserve and to remove your rivals harmlessly is a course that must be practiced while reaching maturity.

Mi Heng (AD 173 – 198), courtesy name Zhengping, is an ancient Chinese writer and musician who lived in the late Eastern Han Dynasty. His fu rhapsody "Fu on the Parrot" is the only work that has survived to modern times. Although Mi was known as a gifted poet and talented writer, he was prone to erratic behavior, offensive jokes, and an arrogant attitude that made him difficult to socialise with, and even caused some to question his sanity.

Upon arriving in Xuchang around 196, Kong Rong, minister steward for Xu Commandery, truly appreciated Mi's talent and recommended him to the warlord Cao Cao, who later summoned him for an audience. However, having a low opinion of Cao, Mi refused to attend. Cao was outraged with Mi's refusal, but refrained from punishing Mi due to his reputation as a talent. Knowing Mi was also a talented drummer, Cao invited him to perform with several other musicians at a banquet. Cao offered special garments for the musicians to wear, but Mi rejected while performing in front of Cao and his guests. When an attendant scolded him for not dressing appropriately, Mi slowly stripped, stood naked for a few moments, and then slowly put on the garment and continued performing without showing any embarrassment. Kong arranged a second meeting between Mi and Cao, but Mi turned out to be as equally as offensive as before, so Cao sent him back to Liu Biao, the warlord of Shu.

Among Liu's subordinates, Mi was highly respected for his literary talent. However, he also criticised Liu for being indecisive and offended most of Liu's other attendants with his arrogant attitude. Liu Biao tolerated him for a year before sending him to Jiangxia Commandery to serve its Administrator, Huang Zu, who was also initially impressed by Mi Heng's intelligence and talent. However, Mi got into trouble when he insulted Huang in front of his guests at a banquet. Huang was outraged and ordered Mi's execution, which was quickly carried out by a senior clerk who hated Mi.

Mi was so annoying that Cao wanted to have him removed, he couldn't do it himself or otherwise fell into the notoriety of killing the wise, so he euphemistically sent Mi to Liu, who then transferred him to Huang, resulting in the death of Mi. As a Chinese proverb says, "killing two birds with one stone", Cao's ruse not only removed Mi with a borrowed knife but also discredited his opponent Liu.

Stratagem 4 · Wait at Leisure While the Enemy Labors

Sun Tzu said: It is advantageous to choose the time and place for battle while the enemy does not. Have your troops well-prepared for battle, at the same time that the enemy is rushing to fight against you, ideally encouraging the enemy to waste energy and resources while you conserve yours. When they are confused and exhausted, then attack them.

Cao Kui's Debate

In the spring of 684 BC, Duke Huan of Qi ordered his army to attack Lu. Cao Gui was appointed as General of Lu to defend the state. Duke Zhuang of Lu also presented at the frontline along with Cao. Cao asked his army to stand still in the battle formation and fortifications and not to fight back until his order. The army of Qi charged twice but the army of Lu stayed in the fortifications and did not respond. When the Qi soldiers started their third charge, Cao ordered his army to launch a counter attack. At this point, soldiers of Qi were tired and could hardly concentrate, so they were defeated. Duke Zhuang immediately ordered his men to chase the fleeing Qi army. Cao accepted the order after making sure that there was no ambush. In the end, the Qi army was thoroughly destroyed and expelled out of the border.

Later, when the Duke asked for an explanation of the success, Gui replied: "The victory in battle lies on the morale of soldiers. At the first drum beat (i.e., order to charge), the morale of Qi soldiers was raised. On the second time, it declined. Finally, on the third time, it had been exhausted. The morale of Qi soldiers was exhausted while our soldiers still brimmed. Consequently we defeated them. This is so-called 'wait at leisure while the enemy labors'".

Coping with Shifting Situations

Keep in mind, waiting at leisure while the enemy labors is also an effective strategy that will keep your organization safe under certain circumstances. In today's incredibly fast paced markets and operating environments, organizations cannot win forever in competition. When the conditions are downright tough, return to rest, recuperate and build up strength, avoiding head-on confrontations with your opponents.

Make feasible plans and take effective measures to adapt more sustainably to the rapidly shifting landscape, avoid what is strong and strike at what is weak. Apply stress and send signals that you are to counterattack without actually doing so, keep them guessing and they will run out of mental energy and so be more likely to make mistakes. When the opponent's resource allocation is weak and its resistance is feeble, it's the best time to attack and attain your true needs.

Stratagem 5 · Loot a Burning House

Sun Tzu said: When a country is beset by internal problems, such as disease, famine, corruption, and crime, it's unable to deal with an outside threat. If the enemy is in its weakest state, attack them without mercy and annihilate them to prevent future troubles.

In specificity, the best time to attack an opponent is when they have their own problems to deal with. Though he who loots a burning house should be careful lest he become trapped inside. In other words, hit your enemy when he is down.

Guanyin Temple Disaster

This proverb originated from the story of Journey to the West. Xuanzang and his disciples embarked on a pilgrimage to India to obtain Buddhist scriptures. They passed through a Guanyin temple on the way to their destination. The abbot hospitably served them. He requested to borrow Xuanzang's beautiful cassock to get a better look and the latter agreed. Late at night, the abbot bolted the door when Xuanzang and his disciples fell asleep, and then set the bedroom on fire. Meanwhile, the Monkey King had stayed awake as he suspected the intention of the abbot. To spoil the abbot's scheme, he transformed himself into a honeybee and lingered outside. The Monkey King blew a strong puff of wind.

The blaze spread over the entire temple and all the monks rushed out to extinguish the flames. At the time, a black bear monster came over and concealed the cassock under the shield of the fire. Although the Monkey King had severely penalized the black-hearted abbot, he lost the master's cassock once again. With no idea of its current possessor or how to reclaim it, he turned to the Bodhisattva Guanyin for assistance. She helped him defeat the black monster and finally acquired the cassock.

Win in Chaos

There are two ways to loot a burning house: One is robbery on fire, the other is arson. The former tries to catch the fish in troubled waters, while the latter attempts to achieve his ulterior purpose after setting the fire.

It sounds somewhat evil when we talk about "looting a burning house", but from a positive standpoint, it essentially means following the trend, namely, behaving harmonically in a completely natural, uncontrived way to achieve one's goals.

In today's highly competitive society, it's an unspoken rule and a necessary skill for professionals in the workplace. As it is said, there are no permanent friends, only permanent interests in the world. Opportunities are won by yourself, fight for reasonable rights and interests you deserve. Great opportunities don't come everyday — recognize and seize the moment for greatness.

Stratagem 6 · Clamor in the East, Then Strike in the West

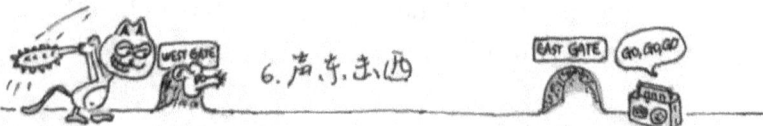

Sun Tzu said: In any battle the element of surprise can provide an overwhelming advantage. Even when you come face-to-face with an enemy, surprise can still be employed by attacking where he least expects it. To do this you must create an expectation in the enemy's mind through the use of a feint. Draw their attention somewhere before attacking elsewhere that is poorly defended. Tactically, this is known as an "open feint".

Recapture of Taiwan by Zheng Chenggong

On April 21, 1661, Zheng Chenggong led an army of 25,000 soldiers and more than 400 warships to set out against the south wind from Liaoluo Bay, Jinmen. To get the enemy to focus its forces elsewhere, Zheng sent out some warships to pretend to attack from the south waterway. Zheng asked the soldiers to beat drums and shout while the artillery was constantly firing, which successfully attracted the attention of the Dutch colonial army to the south waterway. The Dutch captain Thomas Bedell hurriedly mobilized a large number of troops to defend the channel.

While the battle on the south waterway was fierce, Zheng ordered the main warships to march towards Zeelandia in secret. Having overcome the bad weather at sea and lack of food along the way, his troops managed to make landfall through Luer Gate waterway and Heliao Port on April 30 by making use of the astronomical spring tide. The soldiers of the colonial army woke up from dreams perceiving that they had been surrounded. On May 4, Zheng successfully recovered Chiqian City, one of the two Dutch forts in Taiwan. He then laid siege to Zeelandia for more than nine months. During this period, he fought back the reinforcements sent by the Dutch colonists from Batavia and rejected the request of the Dutch invaders who tried to bribe him a withdrawal. In January 1662, Zheng's army recaptured Utrecht outside Taiwan, forcing the Dutch colonists to surrender and sign the Treaty of Peace. This ended the 38-year Dutch rule on Taiwan.

This stratagem is often used by some parties that offer something petty to the audience drawing their attention somewhere and then make them pay dearly. Therefore, be smart to guard yourself not to be fooled by the ruse.

Purloin Silks

Once there was an official who traveled to the capital. The front part of the inn where he stayed was a teahouse, and across the street was a shop selling expensive dyed silks. Whenever he had nothing to do, he would sit by a window in the teahouse watching people come and go on the street. One day, to his surprise, he noticed that several hoodies were walking back and forth observing the silk shop with great interest.

One of them walked up to his table and whispered: "We're burglars with intent to commit a theft at the silk shop. Since you have noticed us, I come to ask you not to report it."

"That has nothing to do with me," the official replied. "Why should I say anything about it?"

The fellow thanked him and left. The official looked at the sky and murmured: 'The silk shop has its wares openly displayed on a busy street. At daylight, with a thousand eyes watching, if they have the skill to purloin the silks, then they must be smart thieves indeed." So he watched carefully to see how they would manage to take it. But what he saw was only the same people walking back and forth in front of the silk shop. Sometimes they gathered on the left, sometimes on the right.

The official sat watching until after sunset when everyone had gone and the shop had closed. "Those fools." said the official to himself. "How would they manage to steal the fine silks?" When he returned to his room to order some food, he discovered that all his belongings were gone.

Stratagem 7 · Create Something from Nothing

Sun Tzu said: You use the same feint twice. Having reacted to the first and often the second feint as well, the enemy will be hesitant to react to a third feint. Therefore, the third feint is the actual attack catching your enemy with his guard down. Tactically, this is known as a "plain lie", i.e., make somebody believe there is something when there is in fact nothing or vice versa.

Zhang Yi Deceived Chu

Zhang Yi (before 329 BC – 309 BC) was born in the Wei state during the Warring States period. He was an important strategist who helped Qin dissolve the unity of the other states, and hence paved the way for Qin to unify China. He was an advocate of horizontal alliance.

At that time, Su Qin's vertical alliance tactic still influenced China, and formed a sort of unity between the states of Han, Zhao, Wei, Chu, Yan and Qi. When Zhang met Duke Huiwen of Qin at the first time, he presented ideas to the duke about measures to befriend Wei and Yan in order to break the alliance, Huiwen was overjoyed and appointed him as the prime minister of Qin.

In 314 BC, Cracks appeared in the alliance. King Huai of Chu, who was the head of the vertical alliance, planned to unite the forces of Chu and Qi to launch an attack at Yan. In fear of the great threat from the Chu-Qi alliance, Huiwen sent Zhang to sow discord among them. Zhang first drew the attention of Huai by bestowing expensive gifts to his favoured official, Jin Shang. He then struck a deal with Huai. They agreed that Huai would end his alliance with Qi if Qin gave back 600 li of land that Qin had previously captured from Chu. Huai promptly accepted Zhang's proposal despite his official Chen Zhen's sneaking suspicion regarding the trustworthiness of Zhang.

Chu unilaterally withdrew from the Chu-Qi alliance. When Huai sent a messenger to Qin's capital Xianyang to retrieve the land, Zhang gave Chu six li of his own land, claiming that he had said 'six li' of his own land instead of the six hundred of Qin he had promised. Chu immediately went to battle with Qin but was defeated and lost a further six hundred li of land.

Zhang repeatedly negotiated with Han, Zhao, Wei, Chu, Yan and Qi, sowed discord among the six states, and thereby destroyed their relationships with horizontal alliance, paving the way for Qin's unification of China.

There are two conditions to be noted in the use of "create something from nothing": (1) the feint you made must look like real; (2) the other party must think the feint you made is true due to the information asymmetry. Only when these two conditions are met, the use of the stratagem can come true. Otherwise, the other party may dissolve the ruse once they eliminate the information asymmetry.

Give an Inch, Take a Mile

A local textile company wanted to import equipment from a Japanese company. Lucas, the local rep, was sent to the Japanese business premise to meet Kentaro, the Japanese rep. After 3 hours of exhausting negotiation, Kentaro was furious: "Lucas, I have consulted our CEO several times and promised to lower our asking price four times, from $2.4 million to $1.2 million, which is 50% lower than the original asking price. Although our benevolence has been utterly exhausted, you haven't yet signed. This conversation sounded tinny and insincere!" He threw his handbag onto the table, burning with anger.

Lucas stood up. "With a lot of suppliers out there, the quoted price and the way you settled are not the best." said Lucas in a tranquil tone of voice, flinging his handbag onto the table as well with a touch of frustration in his eyes.

The bag intentionally failed to zip the chain. Being flung, the equipment information and photos of a certain western company inside were scattered all over the floor. Upon seeing this, Kentaro was shocked. He hurriedly grabbed Lucas with a smile on his face and said: "Wait a moment, Sir. Let me contact my boss now before we discuss further."

"Please tell your boss, we are not interested in such a price you asked." replied Lucas without yielding an inch. He waved his hand and left.

As expected, a message came early the next morning that the Japanese side asked the textile company not to negotiate with other suppliers, and they accepted to lower the asking price to $1.1 million.

In this case, Lucas deliberately kept his handbag unzipped, and the information and photos scattered on the floor were real which engendered an illusion for Japanese side: Aside from the Japanese supplier, there were also other suppliers engaged in the negotiations.

As said above, information asymmetry is the key to the use of the stratagem, namely, the other party cannot verify what you said is false or the cost of verification is too high, or it is too late to do so. To identify this kind of scheme, negotiators must take the initiative to understand the market in advance, to inquire into the "facts" said by the negotiating opponent and verify whether these "facts" are true or not, thus avoiding information asymmetry.

Stratagem 8 · Sneak Through the Passage of Chencang

Sun Tzu said: Deceive the enemy with an obvious approach that will take a very long time, while ambushing them with another approach. It is an extension of the tactic "Make a sound in the east, then strike in the west", but instead of merely spreading misinformation to draw the enemy's attention, physical decoys are used to further misdirect the enemy. The decoys must be easily seen by the enemy to draw their attention while acting as if they are meant to do what they are falsely doing to avoid suspicion.

The Chu–Han Contention

The Chu–Han Contention (206–202 BC) was an interregnum period between the Qin dynasty and the Han dynasty in Chinese history. Han Xin was a military general who served Liu Bang during the Chu–Han Contention and contributed greatly to the founding of the Han dynasty. Han Xin was named as one of the "three heroes of the early Han dynasty", along with Zhang Liang and Xiao He.

After his appointment, Han analysed the situation and devised a ruse for Liu to conquer Xiang Yu's Western Chu kingdom. In late 206 BC, the Han forces left Hanzhong and prepared to attack the

Three Qins in Guanzhong. Han ordered some soldiers to pretend to repair the plank roads linking Guanzhong and Hanzhong while sending another army to secretly pass through Chencang and raid on Zhang Han's forces. Zhang was caught off guard and the Han forces proceeded to take over Sima Xin and Dong Yi's kingdoms, laying the foundation of victory of Han over Chu.

Today's business world is highly competitive, "sneak through the passage of Chencang" is a common stratagem used by merchants who may present false appearances to confuse opponents or attract customers. However, when you use this trick, you must "clearly repair the plank roads" in advance to engender a false appearance without letting your opponents or customers see the flaws before you realize your plan.

The Oil Magnate Armand Hammer

As we all know, the most successful moment in Hamer's business career is in Libya. His is the man for whom the Occidental Petroleum's 30,000 employees and 350,000 shareholders have the greatest admiration.

During the reign of King Idris, Libya attracted oil capitalists from all over the world just like Texas did when oil was first discovered. When Occidental Petroleum came to Libya, it was just as the Libyan government was preparing for the second round of negotiations on the leasing of its land. According to the Libyan laws, oil companies should develop their leased land as soon as possible. If oil cannot be explored, part of the leased land must be returned to the Libyan government.

More than 40 companies from 9 countries participated in this round of bidding. Having researched the culture and protocol of Libya to get some insight into how to conduct business with the King, in the subsequent bid, Hammer deployed the stratagem "sneak through the passage of Chencang" in a different way: Hammer personally submitted Occidental's oil proposal to King Idris on rolled-up sheepskin — the traditional way agreements were executed by tribes in Libya. The cover of the proposal was decorated in three colors: red, green, and green, representing the colors of the Libyan national flag. Meanwhile, the agreement also included unique content that went beyond a standard proposal. For example, Occidental promised to develop agriculture and search for water in Libya.

In March 1966, the presentation and content of Hammer's proposal resonated with the King who said in his own way "I like this guy" and awarded the oil concession to Occidental. Knowing of Hammer's success in obtaining Libyan oil assets, the prominent competitors were thoroughly impressed with his superb negotiation skills and the method he took.

Stratagem 9 · Observe the Fire from the Opposite Shore

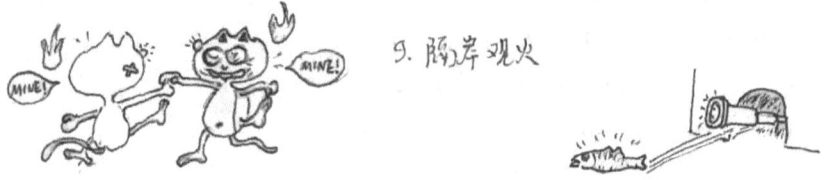

Sun Tzu said: Delay entering the battlefield until all the other parties become exhausted fighting amongst themselves. Then go in at full strength and pick up the pieces.

Also common known as "sit on the mountain and watch the tigers fight", which depicts a situation where you are in a safe position whereas others are fighting for their survival. When discords appear amongst the enemy, restrain yourself from being drawn into the fray. Stand still, let them kill each other, weaken their strengths, or even disintegrate themselves. Either the goal will reveal itself petty as not worth fighting for, or you can attain it later with far less effort.

Cao Cao Wiped out Yuan

At the end of the Eastern Han dynasty, the warlord Cao Cao defeated his rival Yuan Shao at the Battle of Guandu in 200. Yuan Shao died two years later and his sons Yuan Tan and Yuan Shang started fighting each other for control over their father's vast domain. Cao defeated Yuan brothers at the Battle of Liyang in 202–203 and won several consecutive battles. At the time, many of Cao's generals urged Cao to take advantage of his success to continue attacking the Yuans.

Then one of his ministers, Guo Jia, said, "Yuan Shao loved both sons so he couldn't decide between them who would succeed him. With advisers like Guo Tu and Pang Ji to assist the Yuans, internal conflicts will break out between them for sure. If we continue our attacks, the Yuans will unite to resist us. If we withdraw our forces, they will start fighting among themselves. Let us bide our time and allow them to resume fighting each other. After they have weakened themselves we can strike again."

Cao accepted Guo's proposal and withdrew his army to the south. Internal conflicts did break out between the Yuans later, which resulted in Yuan Tan being defeated by his younger brother. Yuan Tan retreated to Pingyuan and sent Xin Pi to meet Cao, agreeing to surrender to Cao and requesting for assistance in dealing with Yuan Shang. Cao led his forces north and defeated Yuan Shang at the Battle of Ye in 204. At this point Cao, having no more use for the alliance, accused Yuan Tan of not doing his part in the siege of Ye and only seeking to further his own ends. The accusation was followed by the cancellation of the alliance. In 205, Cao attacked Yuan Tan and defeated him at the Battle of Nanpi. By then, Cao had pacified most of Ji Province in northern China.

Note that, adopting a "wait-and-see" attitude is the key to the use of the stratagem, you shouldn't wait passively, but take active posture to fully grasp the contradictions amongst the competitors, then accelerate the discord amongst them to satisfy your intention.

Snipe–Clam Grapple

In 1986, Zhuhai Surelink Communication Cable planned to import a set of optical fiber equipment from overseas. After several rounds of research and investigation, they chose to conduct substantive negotiations with ITT Inc, an American worldwide manufacturing company based in White Plains, New York.

All the ITT reps demonstrated high business competency, especially the main negotiator Mohr, whose presentation was eye-catching using rich data and charts. The Surelink reps, however, were undeterred by ITT's imposing manner and did not show any submissiveness. They still sought for a cheaper option.

Surelink understood in the previous investigations that there were many foreign manufacturers who wanted to do optical fiber business with China, therefore, it was completely a buyer's market in a short term due to the continuing fierce competition. So they decided to build a rapport with suppliers, and gain the upper hand in negotiations to attain their own intention.

While negotiating with ITT, Surelink also contacted STC, a British manufacturer of telephone, telecommunications, and related equipment. The two are brother companies. In mid-1982, STC was separated from ITT and became an independent company and was listed on the London Stock Exchange.

For their own interests, the two companies were drawn into the snipe–clam grapple soon. After the second round of negotiation, deliberately, the Britons had two pages of documents left on the negotiating scene for the Americans. In documents the Britons listed an extremely low quote with intent to force the rival to quit. However, the Americans seemed to obtain a treasure after somehow grabbing the documents on the scene, they promptly made further concessions in the subsequent negotiations, and quickly struck the deal with Surelink. In this story, Surelink is the biggest winner who got the best quote from the suppliers saving big money.

Stratagem 10 · Hide Your Dagger Behind a Smile

Sun Tzu said: Charm and ingratiate yourself with your enemy. When you have gained his trust, move against him in secret. In specificity, speak deferentially, listen respectfully, follow his commands, and accord with him in everything. He will never imagine you might be in conflict with him. Your treacherous measures will then be settled.

This stratagem is widely used in business, diplomacy, civilian life and other fields, and it works every time as it hits the most common weakness of humans.

Overwhelmed by Calumnies

Li Yifu was a chancellor of the Tang dynasty during the reign of Emperor Gaozong. He appeared to be mild, humble, and respectful in his temperament, and he was often smiling, but in secret, he was full of treachery and machinations. Therefore, it was said that he had knives in his smile.

In 656, shortly after being granted the title of Marquess of Guangping, Li heard that a Lady Chunyu, from the eastern capital Luoyang, was beautiful, and had been arrested for an offense and held in custody. Li ordered the secretary general of the supreme court, Bi Zhengyi, to set the woman free. Bi followed his order and Li took the woman home.

When this improper release was noticed by the chief judge of the supreme court, he instantly reported to the emperor. On hearing this, Bi, in fear, had to go to Li for help. But Li ignored the thing and asked the man not to disturb him. The poor man was so disappointed that he hanged himself with a piece of cloth.

Another officer Wang Yifang heard about the tragic suicide death of Bi, and wanted to reveal the truth to the emperor. But Li knew his plan and began uttering calumnies against him. The foolish emperor believed Li's words and exiled the officer to a distant area.

A Friend Turned out to Be the Rival

You may often encounter this sort of people in the workplace and in daily life. Here are some tips for identifying those who hide the dagger behind their smile: He generally tends to lower his head, his eyes may shrink and hide without eye contact in conversation. When he laughs, he seems not relaxed enough; his mannerism is frivolous, and most likely you can catch some improper clues in his speech.

Isabella has been depressed for months. She couldn't imagine that her ex-colleague and best friend Claire will openly compete with herself in the same industry. When Claire entered the company, she had no experience in this industry. Isabella, as the director of the department, naturally became her teacher. At that time, Claire was a honey-tongued lady who used to visit Isabella's home during weekends. Isabella is a very humane superior, she never knows how to refuse others' goodwill. For example, Claire often bought some small gifts for her two-year-old son, while Isabella often taught Claire some skills hand over hand.

Two years later, Claire resigned and moved to another company, and she turned out to be Isabella's biggest competitor. As a proverb says, "One who strikes first gains the advantage", she threw out some of the company plans that Isabella had revealed to her, which caught Isabella off guard instantly.

The most taboo thing in the workplace is the confusion of the roles of colleagues and friends, and the confusion between work and private life. In an age where people are driven both by career and personal well being, it's important to recognize when workplace friendships turn into a distraction, ultimately derailing your ability to accomplish your goals. Workplace friendships pose challenges that private, social interactions do not experience. You have to strike a balance between your personal needs and the needs of the workplace for harmony and contribution.

Stratagem 11 · Sacrifice Plums to Preserve Peaches

Sun Tzu said: There are circumstances where short-term objectives must be sacrificed so as to gain the long-term goal. This is the scapegoat strategy whereby someone else suffers the consequences so that the rest do not.

In order to gain one thing it is often necessary to lose another. Trying to hold on to everything at once may cause you in the end to lose everything. Instead, sacrifice smaller concerns to strengthen your more important endeavor.

Sacrifice: The Orphan of Zhao

During the Spring and Autumn period, Tu'an Gu, a traitorous official of the Jin state, wanted to destroy the Zhao family who had made great contributions to Jin. He led 3,000 men to surround Zhao's mansion, killing all the Zhao family, regardless of gender and age. Fortunately, Zhao Shuo's wife, Princess Zhuang Ji, being pregnant, was secretly sent to the palace of the king before the incident. Tu'an then devised a scheme intending to get rid of the newborn baby. When the princess gave birth to a baby boy, Tu'an personally led his men into the palace to search for the baby. At this time, a loyal minister Han Jue asked one of his confidants,

Cheng Ying, to pretend to be a doctor, entered the palace to see the princess, and had the baby hidden in his medicine chest and escaped. Knowing of this, Tu'an threatened to kill every infant in Jin if the Zhao orphan was not produced.

Cheng, in fear, consulted the retired Minister Gongsun Chujiu. To prevent this massacre, Cheng decided to sacrifice his own child in desperation so that the safety of the Zhao orphan and every infant in the state was ensured. Gongsun departed with Cheng's child, whom he presented as the Zhao orphan. Gongsun and the child were sentenced to death immediately. Cheng silently suffered and weeped for his own child before he escaped to the Shouyang Mountain with the Zhao orphan.

Twenty years later, the Zhao orphan, known as Zhao Wu, had reached maturity. After discovering the truth, he killed Tu'an in streets and avenged his family's collapse. He was later reinstated with his family titles and properties.

Magic Formula

Nara, the ancient capital of Japan, is a beautiful city nestled in the green hills. It has developed from a town of commerce in the Edo and Meiji periods to a modern tourist city, due to its large number of historical temples, landmarks and national monuments. Nara city attracts more than a million visitors every year, making it one of Japan's most popular cities.

After this April, swallows came again, they nested in hotels and inns and bred offspring, rendering a warm and pleasant natural landscape in Nara. The hospitable hotel owners and stewards were happy to provide the convenience of nesting for little swallows. However, the cute little swallows were prone to excreted poops casually, fledglings even splashed feces onto windows and into corridors. Although the stewards often cleaned up the stains, swallows always left droppings everywhere, making the tourists very disappointed. The hotel managers knew that there were only two ways to completely remove poops, one was to increase employees, and the other was to drive away swallows. But after a few attempts, those ways didn't seem to work. Not only was swallow poop unsightly, but it could also be a health hazard. More seriously, this became a major problem in the development of Nara's tourism industry affecting the prosperity of the entire scenic spot.

One day, when the manager of Nara Inn was serving a tour group from Taiwan, he occasionally heard a Chinese idiom "sacrifice plums to preserve peaches". After asking for explanation, he realized that it talked about the scapegoat strategy whereby someone else suffered the consequences on behalf of others, which reminded him of the swallow poops that he couldn't deal with, but now he decided to suffer something on swallow's behalf. So he racked his brains to draw up a peculiar note in the name of Little Swallow:

Ladies and gentlemen:

We are little swallows who have just come here from the south to accompany you through the spring. Without the consent of the master, we have built nests here and have children. Our little babies are young and rather ignorant, and our habits are also nasty. We often stain the windows and corridors making you unhappy. We are so sorry and sincerely beg your forgiveness.

There is one more thing we also wanted to beg you, ladies and gentlemen, please don't blame stewards and waitresses. Every day they work pretty hard to clean up the droppings, but it's hard to keep up the rhythm. This is completely our fault, please wait a moment, they will come.

Your friend — Little Swallow

Little Swallow's naive apology always makes the tourists laugh loudly and dissipate their resentment quietly. Whenever they see the droppings left on the windows or in the corridors, they will naturally think of Little Swallow's intimate and funny words, and can't help rocking back and forth while laughing.

In fact, most tourists have a psychological feature, namely, once they get a pleasant feeling, they will quickly forget the tiny unpleasantness of the trip that may occur. The Nara Inn manager's magic formula exactly captures the psychological characteristics of tourists and subtly resolve their dissatisfaction if any, bringing them sweet memories while bidding farewell to the ancient charming city.

Stratagem 12 · Take the Opportunity to Pilfer a Goat

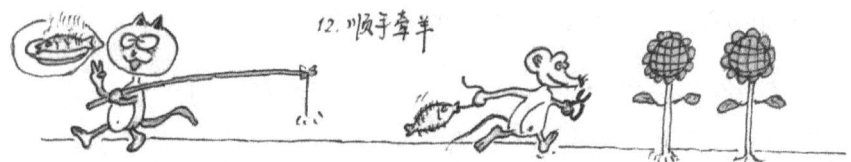

Sun Tzu said: While carrying out your plans, be flexible enough to take advantage of any opportunity that presents itself, however small, and avail yourself of any profit, however slight. A good commander will never lose sight of gains, and he will never doubt when encountering the chances. As long as you do not "lost big due to small gains", the chance of small wins should not be let go. Keep in mind, while following the rules of strategy and tactics be prepared to take advantage of circumstances not covered by conventional thinking. If opportunities present themselves, then the commander should be flexible in his plans and adapt to the new circumstances.

Destroyed a Country at His Leisure

In the winter of 628 BC, Duke Wen of Zheng just passed away while Duke Wen of Jin, the warlord of the Central Plains, was old and weak. Duke Mu of Qin thought that the chance was coming, so he decided to attack Zheng to expand his power in the Central Plains.

In February of the following year, led by General Meng Mingshi, the Qin army passed through the Xiao Mountain and entered the

Hua state adjacent to the Zheng state. At this time, it happened that a businessman named Xian Gao in Zheng drove a group of cows to Luoyi to do business. After he came to Hua and heard that the Qin army was going to attack Zheng, he felt extremely anxious.

Xian thought: My country is holding the national funeral, and there is no preparation at all. If Qin fights over, my country must suffer a big loss.

So he promptly sent a messenger back to Zheng to report the news, he himself pretended to be an envoy of Zheng and approached the Qin army camp with the intention of meeting the young generals of Qin.

On hearing the visit of Zheng's envoy, Meng and his subordinates were very surprised. They walked up to the envoy.

"Hi Sir, welcome here! May I get your name, please?" Meng asked.

"I'm little Xian. Our king heard that your honour led the troops to our country, so he asked me to bring gifts and greetings to your army here. Although our country is not very rich, we are willing to serve your army. If your troops are stationed in our country, we can offer provisions; or if you want to pass by our country, we can send people to guard your troops by your side." said Xian solemnly.

He then brought over twelve fat cows and said to Meng with a smile: "These are the tiny reward for the soldiers, please accept it."

On hearing this, Meng thought Zheng must have been fully prepared in advance, so he thanked Xian and ushered him away. After Xian left, Meng hurriedly sent out his scouts to Zheng to gain information, and found that all cities of Zheng were garrisoned by troops with deep defensive lines. It turned out that Zheng's monarch instantly made careful arrangements after receiving the report. Meng knew that it was impossible to attack Zheng anymore, so he ordered the withdrawal of troops.

"Am I going to retreat with bare hands?" said Meng sadly to himself on the way back. He scratched his ears and murmured: "In this case, let's attack the Hua state, take it down and bring more properties back, so I can explain to the king."

Then he ordered his army to attack Hua. Hua was a small vassal state, without preparation, it was wiped out within a few days.

Never Too Late to Mend the Fold

Precautions to be taken against the stratagem "take the opportunity to pilfer a goat":

1) Avoid loopholes. The main reason why the opponents can easily apply the ruse is that they take advantage of your loopholes. If you can make fewer or no loopholes, then they will have no chance. Be sure to avoid loopholes in your plans and organization.

2) Mend the fold after a goat is lost. Once a loophole appears, it must be immediately remedied. It's not too late to mend the fold after a goat is lost, otherwise all the remaining goats will be lost. Therefore, after discovering the problem, do not hesitate to fix it, and do not rely on fluke or be too lazy to do it.

3) Do not give up small profits. Avail yourself of any profit, however slight, as long as you do not "lost big due to small gains". For your own "goat", you must be aware and take care of it all the time so that it won't get lost.

4) Suspects must be guarded. Before pilfering a goat, the person often has to look around with the sneaky appearance and behavior in fear of being discovered. When he approaches the flock, you should warn him and take strict precautions to stop his attempts.

Stratagem 13 · Stomp the Grass to Startle the Snake

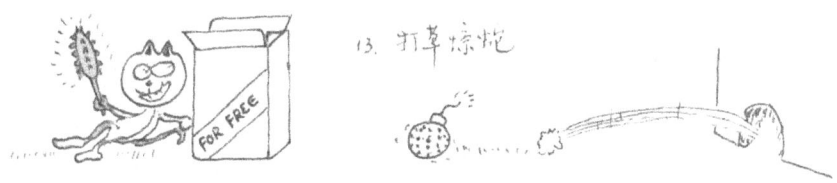

Sun Tzu said: Do something unaimed, but spectacular ("stomping the grass") to provoke a response from the enemy ("startle the snake") to have them give away their plans or position. Do something strange, unusual, and unexpected to arouse the enemy's suspicion and disrupt their thinking. It is more widely used as a warning: "[Do not] startle the snake by beating the grass". An imprudent act will give one's position or intention away to the enemy.

Lure the Snake out of Hiding

In the Spring and Autumn period, the Jiao state was a small vassal country, but it was easy to defend and hard to attack as the walls of its capital, Yun city, were thick and solid. The Chu state, one of the five hegemons of the era, attempted several frontal assaults against Jiao several times but all failed.

Mo'ao, a general of Chu, then devised a ruse. He sent out a platoon of his men to the north of the Yun city, disguising as farmers to chop woods in the mountains, and deliberately disturbing the urban defense forces of Jiao. Jiao dispatched its troops to expel the platoon and captured 30 men.

The next day, Jiao concentrated its superior forces and once again went to the mountains to hunt down the "woodcutters" of Chu. However, they were ambushed on the way and defeated by the Chu army who forthwith conquered the Yun city and destroyed the kingdom of Jiao.

Chrysler: Reckoning to Revival

In the early 1980s, in order to revive Chrysler Automobiles, Lee Iacocca decided to put the bet on convertibles. However, at that time, automobile air conditioning systems and sunroofs were becoming popular, reducing the demand for convertibles. The convertibles almost disappeared as the American automobile industry had stopped producing convertibles for nearly a decade.

Although it was expected that the re-emergence of roofless minivans would arouse the nostalgia of older generations and the curiosity of younger generations, Chrysler had just trudged out of the trough of four consecutive years of losses and could no longer stand any self-inflicted setbacks. For the sake of this, Iacocca decided to adopt the strategy "stomp the grass to startle the snake" to test the market.

Iacocca instructed the workers to manually manufacture a roofless minivan with novel colors and peculiar shapes. It was summer, Iacocca himself drove this convertible minivan on the busy roads.

In the traffic of all sorts of traditional vehicles, the convertible that Iacocca drove seemed to be a monster from an alien planet, attracting a long list of cars that followed. Several luxury cars forced Iacocca's convertible to stop by the roadside, and the followers immediately surrounded Iacocca and asked a series of questions:

"Which company made this car?"

"What brand of car is this?"

....

While answering all questions with smile, Iacocca had a tentative understanding of the sales prospect of convertibles. To further verify, Iacocca drove the minivan to shopping malls, superstores and entertainment centers. Everywhere he went, it always attracted a large crowd to watch and inquire.

Through "beating the grass", Iacocca's sales prospecting was well done. Shortly thereafter, when Chrysler introduced the LeBaron Convertible as a way to make the company stand out from other brands, the LeBaron was expected to sell 3,000 units in its first year, but instead, sold 23,000. Auto makers noticed that convertibles have claimed a slice of the market ever since.

Stratagem 14 · Borrow a Corpse to Resurrect the Soul

Sun Tzu said: Take an institution, a technology, a method, or even an ideology that has been forgotten or discarded and appropriate it for one's own purpose. Revive something from the past or bring to life old ideas, customs, or traditions and reinterpret them to your advantage.

Capture of Jingzhou

During the Three Kingdoms period, Liu Bei's plan to occupy Jingzhou had been around for a long time. In Zhuge Liang's Longzhong plan, he proposed to gain control over Jingzhou so as to secure a viable base for staging attacks against Liu's rival, Cao Cao, and his territories in central and northern China. Therefore, after Liu Bei joined forces with Sun Quan and defeated Cao Cao at Red Cliffs, he couldn't wait to capture Jingzhou and its periphery.

Jingzhou was originally a territory of Liu Biao. When Liu Bei came to Jingzhou the first time, he couldn't control the chaos gripping the territory. The celebrity Ma Liang presented a ruse to Liu Bei: "If your majesty recommends Liu Qi to be the governor of Jingzhou, then the people of Jingzhou will be sincerely convinced. Liu Biao is the former warlord of Jingzhou, and Liu Qi is his son.

Thereby there is no excuse for anyone to riot." Liu Bei accepted his proposal and appointed Liu Qi the governor of Jingzhou. Sure enough, the chaos in Jingzhou quickly settled down. Later, Liu Qi died, and Liu Bei gained full control of the territory.

When Liu Bei just entered Jingzhou, he was not firmly established, so he borrowed Liu Bei's son, Liu Qi, to win people over. Here, Liu Bei borrowed only the name of Liu Qi, and what he wanted to achieve was the long-term occupation of Jingzhou. Once Liu Bei had a firm foothold, what he borrowed instantly lost its effect.

Brain Platinum

Shi Yuzhu is chairman of Giant Interactive, an online game developer and operator in China. His successful rebranding melatonin as "brain platinum" is a typical business case of "borrowing a corpse to resurrect the soul".

If you've ever spent any time watching Chinese TV over the past decade, you're likely to be familiar with a series of advertisements like this:

"No gifts for this year's holidays, only brain platinum is accepted for gifts."

It's a kind of ads played so often that despite being hated by people, the constant repetition has made the product's slogan one of the most recognized in China.

The predecessor of brain platinum is brain gold that has disappeared in the market. Based on the existing business model of brain gold, Shi and his team repositioned this "health care" product in targeting to the specific customers: the elderly and parents.

Through ads, the audience are encouraged to give boxes of this "brain platinum" to older relatives and friends when they're not sure what else to get them. The medicine is supposed to help people sleep, but nobody is really sure if it actually does that, still, it was once quite a popular gift in China, especially during the Spring Festival.

In this case, you will find an interesting phenomenon that the buyers and users of the product are not the same group. Buyers are gift-giving people, usually children, relatives, and friends, who pay for the product; while users are parents or elders, who are the recipients of the product and ultimately use it.

Shi may not care about the topic of melatonin and human health. The first thing consumers think about when they give gifts is whether he is the first one. After all, melatonin is just an optional gift for consumers, but for the giant it is the key to deciding whether to escape the "primary loss" abyss.

After three years of market operations, melatonin has become very popular in China. As a result, we all saw that after the rebranding, not only did Shi pay off the debts, but also the giant found a new cash flow.

Stratagem 15 · Lure the Tiger off His Den

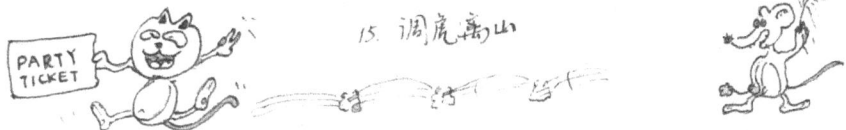

Sun Tzu said: Never directly attack an opponent whose advantage is derived from their position. Instead, lure them away from their position to separate them from their source of strength.

The key to lure the tiger away from his den lies on the word "lure", and the purpose is to get the tiger away from his den. Therefore, the action of "luring" should be ingenious and flexible, and the "tiger" must be allowed to leave his den without making the fake to be coming true, and it bites back.

Capture of Lujiang

At the end of the Eastern Han dynasty, the country was thrown into turmoil by warlords. In his 20s, Sun Ce had consolidated his newly conquered territories in the south and his next goal was the prosperous area of Lujiang to the north. However, Lujiang had a strong army and was well defended. In addition, it also had the advantage of terrain, being accessible only through a couple of easily defended passes. Sun's advisors cautioned against moving directly against such a well-entrenched and powerful state so they devised another scheme.

Knowing that Liu Xun, the warlord of Lujiang, was extremely greedy, Sun sent him a precious gift with a letter praising his achievements and kindly asking for him in support of conquering Shangliao, a rich area that Liu wanted to take it long ago. Considering that Sun was weak and incompetent, Liu disregarded the advice of his counselors and attacked Shangliao.

Several weeks later, while Liu was busy laying siege to Shangliao's capital, his own territory was almost undefended. Sun was overjoyed and said, "I have lured the tiger out of the mountain, let's hurry up and occupy its nest!" Sun led his army to strike at Lujiang and captured the capital soon.

Without the expected support from Sun, Liu failed to take the capital of Shangliao and he returned only to find his own capital already in enemy hands. Sun now had the advantage of the Lujiang terrain and the poor former warlord could do nothing but flee with his army.

KFC China: Regain Reputation After Food Safety Scares

In 2005, many of KFC's product were found of using an illegal chemical substance called Sudan dye as toner. Although it had placed some negative impact on KFC's reputation, many people started to come back after a few months. It seemed that people had already healed wounds and forgot pains, leading KFC's regaining of its top position soon in the fast food market.

Looking back on this incident, we noticed that in the process of KFC's crisis management, KFC's parent company, US-based Yum Brands had been following the pace of government investigations, and even conducted "self-examination and self-correction" concurrently, striving to lock all suppliers to investigate "Sudan I" and its sources. In doing so, Yum not only made consumers feel its attention and determination in resolving the incident, but also allowed consumers to consciously stand by Yum's side and thus shifted the focus of the problem to upstream suppliers. In other words, Yum placed itself on the same "victim" perspective as the public, and lured the tiger (the public) off its den (the problem), which not only weakened the negative image of KFC, but also aroused the sympathy and resonance of the public.

Stratagem 16 · One Must Let Loose in Order to Capture

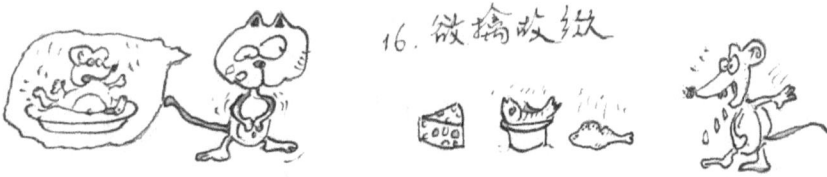

Sun Tzu said: Cornered prey will often mount a final desperate attack. To prevent this, let the enemy believe they still have a chance for freedom. Their will to fight is hampered by their desire to escape. The enemy's morale will be depleted and they will surrender without a fight when the illusion of escape is revealed.

Seven Captures of Meng Huo

Meng Huo was the leader of the Yi people in Nanzhong during the Three Kingdoms period. In 225 AD, he rebelled against Shu. In order to consolidate the rear, Zhuge Liang, the prime minister of the Shu, led his army to march south and subdued the rebellion. When Zhuge was ready to withdraw his troops, Meng gathered the defeated skirmishers to attack the Shu army again. Zhuge knew that Meng was not only brave and strong-willed in combat, but also loyal to others, and he was extremely popular among the Yi people. Even among the Han people, many people admired him, so he decided to win him over.

During the conquest, Meng was captured on seven different occasions by Zhuge. When he was caught for the seventh time, he was convinced by Zhuge and said: "Seven times captured, seven times freed, such a thing has never happened before! Though I stand beyond the range of imperial grace, I am not utterly ignorant of ritual, of what propriety and honour require. No, I am not so shameless!" He then stripped off one of his sleeves (a sign of swearing oath) and pledged: "By the Chancellor's celestial might, the Southerners will never rebel again." Since then, the Nanzhong area had returned to the control of Shu, and Shu maintained a stable state at its rear.

Apple's Acquisition of Intel's Smartphone Modem Business

According to Forbes, Apple and Intel have signed an agreement for Apple to acquire the majority of Intel's smartphone modem business. Approximately 2,200 Intel employees will join Apple, along with intellectual property, equipment and leases. The transaction, valued at $1 billion, is expected to close in the fourth quarter, subject to regulatory approvals and other customary conditions, including works council and other relevant consultations in certain jurisdictions.

When Apple did not reach a settlement with Qualcomm last year, Apple was put in a tough situation when negotiating with Intel to acquire its modem business, because Intel was its only baseband chip supplier at the time. If Intel wanted to sell its modem business, it would definitely ask for a high price. Obviously, this wasn't what Apple expected, the giant was brewing a plot to repeat the routine of acquiring Dialog-related businesses.

Apple first stopped negotiating the purchase of Intel's modem business, and then poached some key personnel in 5G dev from Intel. For example, in February, Apple recruited Umashankar Thyagarajan, senior director of Intel's 5G project, from Intel. Then it settled with Qualcomm and reached a new cooperation, resulting in the plunge of Intel's modem business. Note that in the mobile phone modem market, Apple is the only customer to Intel, and Apple's abandonment means that there are no customers for Intel's mobile phone modems, forcing Intel to announce withdrawal of its modem products on the same day.

Intel is reluctant to invest too heavily not seeing any path for making its money back. The 5G modem business has hemorrhaged money since Intel entered the industry in 2010. Although Intel has been actively seeking to sell its modem business since then, no new takers have appeared.

If Apple jumps out at this time and says: Hi, I'm interested in your modem business, but I won't buy it as a whole. I only want you to be responsible for the relevant technology of the XMM 8160 modem (originally a 5G baseband chip designed for Apple). Can you sell talents and patent authorizations on modems?

In this case, if Intel accepts the bid and strikes a deal, then it will allow Apple to obtain the core talents and patented technology of Intel modems at a very low cost. Even if Intel insists on selling its modem business as a whole, it is difficult to sell at high prices.

Stratagem 17 · Toss out a Brick to Obtain the Jade

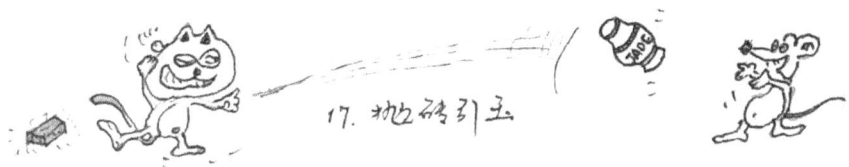

Sun Tzu said: Bait someone by making someone believe he gains something or just make him react to it ("toss out a brick") and obtain something valuable from him in return ("get a jade gem").

To "lure" the enemy, you must first "faze" it, "lure" and "faze" are closely related and indivisible. "Tossing out a brick" is the means while "obtaining the jade" is the goal. The "bricks" thrown out must resemble "jade", which is somewhat a camouflage to show its appearance to the enemy in order to obtain the real jade.

Die for the King

Once upon a time, there was a lady named An lingchan who looked like a goddess and had a graceful posture, and thus won the favor of the King of Chu.

A minister named Jiang Yi visited An and said: "I heard that a person who uses money to deal with others, once his money runs out, people's friendship with him will be alienated; A belle who is pleasing others with her beauty, once she is old and faded, the favor she gets will diminish. Today you are a flower, but the flower will surely wither. How can you make the king love you forever without any revulsion?"

An saluted him and asked: "I am young and ignorant, could you please give me some advice, Sir?"

Jiang said: "Humans cannot revive after death, and there is nothing sadder than this. If you are willing to die for the king in the future, then he will love you forever."

An nodded and said, "That sounds great! I will follow your advice, Sir."

One day, the king took An out hunting. Suddenly, a mad rhino rushed towards the king, and the archer next to him shot and killed the rhino with arrow. "This hunting trip has an indelible happy end." said the king, but suddenly, his face turned gloomy, "Time passes quickly like a white pony's shadow across a crevice, what will happen after one hundred years?"

Sensing that the chance had come, An knelt in front of the king and wept: "After your majesty, I, your servant, is willing to be buried with."

On hearing this, the king was deeply moved, and instantly granted her a fief as a reward.

In this story, the promise of An's burial is a "brick", and the favor of the king and the fief granted are the "jade" brought by the "brick".

Shaw Mobile Has Arrived

In the business arena, the stratagem "toss out a brick to obtain the jade" can be extended and interpreted as: use discounts, coupons, or perks to attract more potential customers, and make them act pursuant to one's wishes. Similarly to "give first, take later", one spends a small amount of money and gives up some benefits first, so as to win customers over gaining larger market share.

Building on the strength of its Fibre+ network, Shaw Communications has recently introduced its 'Shaw Mobile Has Arrived: Brighter Together' advertising campaign across Canada, promulgating that Shaw Internet customers in B.C. and Alberta can now add wireless to their Shaw Fibre+ Internet to get as many as six lines of unlimited nationwide talk and text for $0 monthly.

"Shaw Mobile customers will get the most cost-effective wireless experience in Canada by taking full advantage of our Fast LTE and our WiFi service, powered by Shaw Fibre+," said Brad Shaw, Executive Chair and CEO, Shaw Communications. "We are pleased to deliver what Canadians have wanted from their wireless carriers for years — innovation and technology that helps them save money without sacrificing connectivity."

Shaw Mobile is designed around the fact that Canadians have been increasingly choosing to reduce their monthly wireless costs by using their smartphones on WiFi rather than cellular data. This long-term trend has been driven by the dramatic growth in the number of WiFi hotspots, the number of devices capable of connecting to WiFi, and more recently, the movement toward working from home.

Stratagem 18 · To Defeat the Bandits, Capture Their Leader

Sun Tzu said: If the enemy's army is strong but is allied to the commander only by money or threats, then take aim at the leader. If the commander falls, the rest of the army will disperse or come over to your side. If, however, they are allied to the commander through loyalty, then beware, the army can continue to fight on after his death out of vengeance. Thereby, loyalty is powerful.

Deploy a detachment of shock troops and select commandos to focus their assault on the enemy's vital points. This is the way to slay their commanders.

Battle of Suiyang

During the An Lushan Rebellion in the Tang dynasty, the rebel commander Yin Ziqi led his army to besiege Suiyang city. The defending commander, Zhang Xun, noticed that Yin oversaw the siege from outside the range of the city's archers. He believed that if he could take out the commander the rebel's morale would sink and he would be able to stage a counter attack. He devised a plan with his best archers.

However, in an age before photography, the problem was that Zhang had no idea what Yin looked like, not to mention he could be in a crowd of soldiers. Zhang therefore turned to psychology. He ordered his troops to shoot branches of trees, instead of arrows, at a few enemy soldiers. When these soldiers noticed that they were being shot by branches of trees, hence were not killed, they were overjoyed. They promptly ran to Yin reporting that the Tang army had already run out of arrows. Zhang noticed where the soldiers ran and ordered his best archers to shoot at Yin. One such arrow hit Yin in his left eye, throwing the rebel army into chaos consequently. With this major blow to the rebel morale, the siege to the Suiyang city eventually collapsed.

Grasp the Key Points

In business operations, the stratagem "to defeat the bandits, capture their leader" can be extended and interpreted as: firmly grasp the key to the development and evolution of things, or grasp the key points of problems incurred.

Today's business world is highly crowded and competitive. When developing new products, you should develop winning products using top-notch technologies in order to stand out from the rest of competitors. While promoting your sales, you should analyse the consumer psychology and demographics so as to catch the main consumer groups, suit their needs and preferences through the improvement of the quality, style and packaging of products.

The road to success is not a straight line. If you look at the world-renowned entrepreneurs, such as John D. Rockefeller, Andrew Carnegie, Yue-Kong Pao, Henry Ford, etc. you may find that they all started by focusing on operating a certain industry, and they are all famous for their operations or manufacturing of certain products in specific fields. Therefore, enterprise operators, especially small and medium-sized enterprises, must concentrate human, material and financial resources in their operations. As for large enterprises engaging in diversified or multi-faceted operations, each step of operations must be carefully studied so as to concentrate on grasping the key points.

Stratagem 19 · Remove the Firewood from Under the Pot

Sun Tzu said: Take out the leading argument or asset of your target, denying your enemy the resources needed to oppose you. When faced with an enemy too powerful to engage directly, you must first weaken him by undermining his foundation and attacking his source of power. Literally, take the fuel out of the fire.

Raid on Wuchao

In the Battle of Guandu in 200 AD, Cao Cao led his army of less than 20,000 men to confront Yuan Shao's army boasted of numbers up to 110,000. Cao followed a decisive advice and raided Wuchao, an important supply depot of Yuan. This turned the situation of the battle, and Cao finally defeated his formidable rival, gaining the control of the Central Plains of China.

Guandu was far from Yecheng, Yuan's base camp, elongating Yuan's logistics supply line to the front. Worse still, this supply line had to cross the Yellow River to deploy provisioning, making the transportation of materials across rivers costly and inefficient in absence of bridges. Even though Yuan had controlled a lot grain-producing areas at that time, it was hard to maintain long-term cross-river transhipment, therefore, Yuan chose Wuchao, located at the south of the Yellow River, as the supply depot. The provisions of Yuan were first transported to Wuchao for storage, and then sent to the front at Guandu. Since the southern region of the Yellow River was under the dominance of Cao, the Wuchao base naturally became a pain point of Yuan's army.

Defected over to Cao, Xu You, an advisor previously served for Yuan, presented Cao a proposal to attack Wuchao. Although the proposal was opposed by Cao's subordinates thinking that Wuchao was firmly guarded by Yuan's 10,000 men, Cao eventually accepted it. After all, as it's said: if you don't gamble today, you won't have the chance to gamble tomorrow.

At night, Cao led 5,000 infantry and cavalry to attack Wuchao after leaving Cao Hong and Xun You in charge of his main camp at Guandu. Cao's army disguised itself as a reinforcement unit from Yuan, sortied Wuchao and set on fire. The raid on Wuchao was a great success, inflicting over a thousand casualties of Yuan. Almost all of Yuan's food supplies at Wuchao were burnt. By dawn, Wuchao had turned into an inferno and the morale of Yuan's army plummeted due to the loss of food supplies. Yuan's numerous troops were destroyed and much of his supplies were captured. Yuan himself fled north across the Yellow River with only about 800 cavalry.

U.S. Immigration Policy: Home for Talents

Within a global context of increasing competition, skilled professionals from one country and one place are often poached by other countries. Being removed the firewood from under the pot, countries experiencing the brain drain are becoming feeble.

After the Second World War, the United States specially revised its immigration laws twice in order to attract talents from foreign countries, and it has successively recruited 220,000 senior professionals of various types from overseas. In addition, the United States has also invested a lot in attracting and training foreign students.

According to a Pew Research Center analysis of U.S. Immigration and Customs Enforcement (ICE), between 2004 and 2016, nearly 1.5 million foreign graduates of U.S. colleges and universities obtained authorization to remain and work in the U.S. through the federal government's Optional Practical Training program (OPT). More than half of the foreign graduates approved for employment specialized in science, technology, engineering and mathematics (STEM) fields.

OPT is one mechanism by which the U.S. can compete with other countries for top talent. It is less well-known than the H-1B visa program – which enables U.S. companies to hire highly skilled foreign workers and is the nation's largest temporary employment visa program – yet OPT approvals actually outnumbered initial H-1B visa approvals in recent years.

Stratagem 20 · Stir up the Water to Catch Fish

Sun Tzu said: Before engaging your enemy's forces create confusion to weaken his perception and judgment. Do something strange, unusual, and unexpected as this will arouse the enemy's suspicion and disrupt his thinking. In chaos when a distracted enemy is more vulnerable, it is easier for you to seize power.

Borrow Arrows With Thatched Boats

During the Three Kingdoms period, when the Wei and Wu kingdoms joined together to fight against the Wei Kingdom. Zhou Yu, the chief military commander of Wu, ordered Zhuge Liang (the chief minister of Shu and generally regarded as the kingdom's top master-mind) to produce 100,000 arrows within 10 days.

"Three days is enough, " said Zhuge. He also agreed to be punished if he failed to complete the order.

Mocking that Zhuge was looking for self-destruction, Zhou ordered his troops not to provide Zhuge with materials to make arrows, and also sent General Lu Su to see how Zhuge was tackling the problem.

In fact, Zhuge had already realized that this was a scheme. He asked Lu, who was kind-hearted, to lend him 20 boats, each lined with straw scarecrows and manned by 30 soldiers. He also requested Lu not to tell Zhou what was happening.

When Lu came again to see Zhuge, he did not find anything unusual. Nothing happened on the second day either. In the early morning of the third day, Zhuge invited Lu for a boat ride. The 20 boats were tied together with strong ropes and the fleet sailed toward the camp of Cao Cao, the warlord of Wei.

At that time, thick mists had spread over the river, and people could hardly see each other within feet. When Zhuge's fleet got close to the Cao camp before dawn, Zhuge ordered the soldiers to shout and beat drums faking an attack. Zhuge and Lu simply sat inside one of the boats and drank wine to enjoy themselves.

As soon as the Cao camp heard the shouting and drum beating, they mistook it for a surprise attack by the Zhou camp. Since they could see nobody on the river, Cao gathered 3,000 archers and ordered them to shoot arrows. The front of the scarecrows was quickly shot full of arrows.

After a while, Zhuge had his fleet turn around to expose the other side of the scarecrows. When this side was also shot full of arrows, the day broke. Zhuge ordered the soldiers to return to their base port. After they got back to their camp, they collected more than 100,000 arrows from the scarecrows.

In this story, Zhuge smartly utilized the heavy mists to catch the fish in troubled waters. The heavy mists over the river are like "troubled waters", and the 100,000 arrows are equivalent to "fish".

Blockchain: Fish and Dragons Jumbled Together

Blockchain burst on the tech scene ten years ago with the launch of Bitcoin. Blockchain tech is regarded as the core impetus that has the most potential to trigger the fifth wave of disruptive revolution after steam engine, electricity, information and internet technology. Historically, when the centralized power of the government and large enterprises is weakened or is about to change, many innovative organizations and business models will emerge, thus creating a huge wealth effect.

While new technologies bring great opportunities, fish and dragons will jumble together in the waters where wealth and opportunity gather. With so many companies engaging in the blockchain tech in recent years, investors must figure out the background of the blockchain related projects before they enter the industry.

Here are some tips for identifying a good blockchain related project:

1) Generally, the background information and details of a blockchain project can be found in its official website or in the white paper. Firstly, you need to verify whether or not the information of the project team members is falsified. Secondly, you should check whether or not the official website has been launched hurriedly or presented recently. If there are any discrepancies or inconsistencies in its description, you need to be more vigilant.

In addition, when a cryptocurrency startup wants to raise money through ICO, it usually creates a whitepaper which outlines what the project is about, the goal the project will achieve upon completion, how much money is needed, how many of the virtual tokens the founders will keep, what type of money will be accepted, and how long the ICO campaign will run for.

2) A blockchain project must serve an actual purpose, one that makes sense and is clearly useful in some way. For instance, blockchain + field, specifically, blockchain + finance, aiming to solve the problem of financial payment transactions. Blockchain + academic research, aiming to solve the problem of academic frauds, and to reduce the cost of manual verification and paper costs. Blockchain + election, the use of blockchain tech + voting can truly implement a transparent election process, in which the voter's voting record won't be tampered with. Blockchain + automobile, etc.

3) As mandated by the U.S. Securities and Exchange Commission (SEC), the white paper of a blockchain project should also contain a statement disclaimer, covering "forward-looking statements" about the company's future revenues, organic growth, token flows, token conversions, pension funding contributions, and earnings per token/share, etc.

4) Whether the core tech used for the blockchain project is innovative and how it will surmount the technological challenges that may incur. If it's open source, whether it's actually decentralised that won't come with a ton of 'owners'. The option of which blockchain (eg. bitcoin or ethereum) is based for development onwards and its consensum mechanism must also be detailed in its website or white paper.

5) Analyze the team members to see if there is an adept (top talent) in the team. Aside from this, see whether the team structure is scientific, namely, it should contain legal consultants, industry consultants, project management committees, third-party agencies, etc.

Stratagem 21 · Slough off the Cicada's Golden Shell

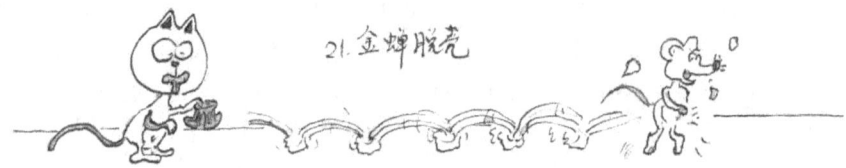

Sun Tzu said: When you are in danger of being defeated by a strong enemy, and your only chance is to escape and regroup, then mask yourself and create an illusion. While the enemy's attention is focused on this artifice, secretly remove your men leaving behind only the facade of your presence.

It is a well-known rule of war that troops are extremely vulnerable when retreating. A strong blow against the retreating troops usually leads to a rout and slaughter. Whenever you are moving troops, leave behind something that will divert or slow potential pursuers.

Hanging Sheep Beat Drums

During the Kaixi reign of the Song dynasty, Jin kingdom persistently disturbed the Central Plains. One day, Jin mobilized its elite cavalry of 10,000 men and staged an attack the Song army. At this time, the Song army had only 2,000 men, and if they battle against the Jin army head-on, they would definitely lose. Bi Zai, General of Song, prepared to temporarily retreat in order to preserve his strength. The Jin army was already under the city, if they knew that the Song army was retreating, they would definitely hunt down. That way, the Song army must suffer heavy losses.

Upon hearing the sound of horse hoofs outside the tent, Bi was inspired coming up with a ruse. He secretly made the deployment of withdrawal. At midnight, he ordered his soldiers to beat the drums. The Jin army heard the sound of drums, thought that the Song Army was about to launch a sortie at night and hurriedly assembled their troops to prepare for the battle.

The soldiers of Jin only heard the rumbling of the drums, but they didn't see anyone coming out from the city. The Song army continued to beat the drums, making the soldiers of Jin unable to rest all night. The general of Jin seemed to be somewhat enlightened: the Song Army must have been disturbing us by using the strategy of "exhausting the enemy". Well, you beat your drums, I will never be fooled by you again.

Even though the drums rang for two days, all the officials and soldiers of Jin just ignored it. On the third day, the Jin army found that the sound of drums gradually faded. The general of Jin judged that the Song army must have been exhausted, so he sent troops to outflank and cautiously approached the enemy's city. However, there was no response from the city, the Jin army then rushed into the city and realized that the Song army had already evacuated.

It turned out that Bi had ordered his soldiers to tie up the hind legs of dozens of sheep to a tree, and make the front legs of the sheep hanging upside down to desperately kick the drums beneath. Bi and his men evacuated safely within two days.

Grafted Flowers

In business, the stratagem "slough off the cicada's golden shell" usually refers to creating a new company to replace the old one due to poor operation or suspension, and gradually transfer the original assets to the new entity. The old company goes bankrupt and the debt disappears.

After the U.S. and its allies imposed sanctions on Russia's largest oil company Rosneft in February this year, Rosneft closed its oil trading subsidiary Rosneft Trading SA, a new oil trading company Energopole SA was then established.

Rosneft Trading SA was established in 2011, registered in Switzerland, and was responsible for the overseas projects of Rosneft. The U.S. Treasury Department said the company helped Venezuela transport and sell crude oil. The source told Reuters that Energopole SA will assume the main functions previously performed by Rosneft Trading SA, supplying products to Rosneft's refineries and European trading organizations.

A representative of Rosneft testified that Energopole SA is a 100% subsidiary of Rosneft and has nothing to do with Rosneft Trading SA. Energopole was registered in Switzerland as well pursuant hereto applicable laws. Energopole does not intend to conduct any businesses with South American countries.

According to the business and enterprise register website of Swiss Federal Statistical Office (FSO), Energopole was registered in Geneva on March 31. Prior to this, the entity was called Rosneft European Services Group SA.

As stated by sources, Energopole has just started operations and is still conducting clearing procedures with related banks and financial parties. Some former teams of Rosneft Trading SA may move to Energopole, but half of them, especially the management department, are not expected to work for the new entity.

Stratagem 22 · Shut the Door to Catch the Thief

Sun Tzu said: To capture one's enemy, cut off the enemy's escape routes and any routes from external aid, then deliver the final blow to the enemy. Do not rush into action, plan prudently for success. Allowing your enemy to escape will plant the seeds for future conflicts. But if they have already succeeded in escaping, be wary of giving chase.

In military practice, this stratagem is generally deployed in conjunction with other plans. It is roughly equivalent to the commonly used siege and annihilation tactics and pocket formations that military strategists often talk about.

War Is Not a Game

Zhao Kuo (? — 260 BC) was a general of the Zhao state during the Warring States period in ancient China. He lost the epic Battle of Changping between Zhao and Qin in 260 BC.

In the late Warring States period, Qin waged a battle against Zhao. The Zhao army suffered several minor defeats during initial confrontations with the Qin forces. Having assessed the enemy, Lian Po, general of Zhao, decided the only way to defeat Qin was to wait them out, as the battlefield — Changping was far away from

Qin territory making it hard for them to maintain the logistics supply line to the front.

The Zhao army built several fortresses and then waited for the enemy to go away. Qin managed to breach the defenses a few times but all failed; nonetheless, Qin refused to leave. Bai Qi, general of Qin, sent agents into Zhao and Han to spread rumors that Lian was too senile and cowardly to fight. Duke Xiaocheng of Zhao was already dissatisfied with Lian's strategy of dragging out the war, so he had Lian replaced by Zhao Kuo, son of Zhao She, a famous general of Zhao, who had told his wife on his deathbed never to let his son Zhao Kuo command an army, because he thought of war as games and treated it with hubris rather than caution despite no any experience in actual battles.

Zhao Kuo assumed command of an army reinforced to approximately 400,000 men. After he arrived in Changping, he completely changed Lian's strategy of sticking to no fight and advocated a decisive battle against the enemy. He took part of his army and attacked the Qin camp. Bai ordered a withdrawal of his army toward the Qin fortress, drawing Zhao after him. Meanwhile, Bai dispatched a 30,000-man cavalry unit with bows and crossbows to outflank behind and sprang the trap planned.

When Zhao reached the Qin fortress, the Qin cavalry ambushed Zhao's rear while the Qin light cavalry surrounded the Zhao fortress. With the enemy trapped, Bai launched a counterattack. The Zhao army was split in two making its supply lines cut in half. Zhao was unable to continue his attack or return to the Zhao fortress; his army dug in on a hill and stood their ground.

Zhao's hill fortification was besieged for one and a half months. Having run out of food and water and with low morale, his desperate army made several unsuccessful attempts to break out.

Zhao Kuo was killed by Qin archers while leading his shock troops in a final attempt to breach the encirclement. With their commander gone, the Zhao army finally surrendered.

Two points for the use of the stratagem: (1) The "thief" must be allowed to step into the concealed positions, and then the door can be closed. (2) After closing the door, you must use a certain method to catch the thief. In the business arena, there are also many examples regarding "shut the door to catch the thief". To this end, enterprises need to understand the consumer psychology and behavior trends, and then take corresponding measures.

Kindly Step into the Vat

In the 1980s, when Sweden's Scandinavian Airlines (SAS) was in a tough situation, Jan Carlzon was appointed president of the company. At this time, the second oil shock caused the global recession, and SAS had gradually lost its reputation due to two consecutive years of losses. In order to relieve the predicament, Carlzon and his team drew up and implemented a series of reform measures. One of them is to carry out a set of new service standards in the air and on the ground.

One of the first things Carlzon did at SAS was to attract business travelers with high-quality services introducing the world's first separate cabin for Business Class while simultaneously doing away with First Class on its European routes. He analyzed the psychology of people traveling on business and believed that they didn't care about the prices of air tickets because they had to be reimbursed anyway, but they were rather picky about the quality of services provided. As long as the services were good and they were satisfied, they would be conquered psychologically. Hence all cabins located at the front of the aircraft were equipped with spacious leather seats, constituting a comfortable environment to meet the needs of business travelers for ultimate experiences.

Within one year of taking over, SAS had become the most punctual airline in Europe and had started an ongoing training program "Putting People First" focusing on delegating responsibility away from management and allowing customer-facing staff to make decisions to resolve any issues on the spot. Carlzon said at the time: "Problems are solved on the spot, as soon as they arise. No front-line employee has to wait for a supervisor's permission."

In order to further revamp the quality of services, Carlzon also built a service network with 131 hotels in the world. For example, after getting off the plane in London, a passenger taking SAS can hand over his luggage to any SAS check-in counter at the airport. When he arrives at a specified hotel, his luggage is already in the room. When he leaves the hotel, he only needs to hand over his luggage to the SAS business counter in the front lobby of the hotel, get his boarding pass, and board the plane directly.

The measures of high-quality services advocated by Carlzon that cater to passengers' psychology are essentially a specific application of the stratagem "closing the door to catch the thief", i.e. inviting the passengers into the vat. These changes soon impacted the bottom-line of SAS, gradually making it become a world-renowned giant.

Stratagem 23 · Befriend a Distant State While Attacking a Neighbor

Sun Tzu said: It is known that nations that border each other become enemies while nations separated by distance and obstacles make better allies. When you are the strongest in one field, your greatest threat is from the second strongest in your field, not the strongest from another field. Invading neighboring nations carries a higher chance of success since the battlefields are close to your domain and as such it is easier to maintain your supplies.

Unifying the Six States

At the end of the Warring States period, the seven warlords (Qin, Zhao, Wei, Qi, Yan, Chu, Han) fought for hegemony in China. Since Qin started Shang Yang's Reform, it had evolved to become the most powerful of the seven major states. Duke Zhao of Qin wanted to unify the six states and dominate the Central Plains. In 270 BC, Duke Zhao summoned his men in attempting to attack Qi. At this time, Fan Jyu, the prime minister of Qin, presented Duke Zhao a policy of "befriend a distant state while attacking a neighbor" to prevent Duke Zhao from attacking Qi.

Fan Jyu said: Qi is strong and far away from Qin. To attack Qi, our troops must pass through Han and Wei. If we send out fewer troops, it is difficult to win; but even if we send out more troops, we're still unable to occupy the vast land of Qi. Thereby, it is better to attack the neighboring states Han and Wei first and advance gradually.

In order to prevent Qi from forming an alliance with Han and Wei, Duke Zhao promptly sent envoys and formed an alliance with Qi. For over 40 years, Qin Shihuang continued to hold to Fan Jyu's policy. He made distant contacts with Qi and Chu. First, he attacked Han and Wei, and then advanced from the two wings to defeat Zhao and Yan and unified the north. Next, he conquered Chu and subdued the south. Later, he forced Qi to surrender. Qin Shihuang fought for ten years and finally realized his great will of unifying China.

Vertical and Horizontal Strategic Alliance

In the business arena, the stratagem of "befriend a distant state while attacking a neighbor" can be extended and interpreted as: open up a neighboring market or compete with nearby opponents. In order to make the situation beneficial to yourself, the opponents at a distance can also be appropriately combined.

In specificity, from the perspective of time, conforming to market demands, you seek short-term benefits or make long-term plans to maintain a good development momentum; from the perspective of business operations, the stratagem is also applicable to the planning and development of enterprises. If you hurriedly engage in an industry that you are not good at or not familiar with, you will most likely fail, just like fighting far away.

Be aware that a friend of your enemy becomes your enemy while an enemy of your enemy becomes your friend. Every powerful person, organization, or state will automatically create people, groups, and organizations that stand in opposition to it. To undermine any objective, you can enlist the aid of those institutions that are the antithesis of your opponent.

Stratagem 24 · Obtain Safe Passage to Conquer the Guo State

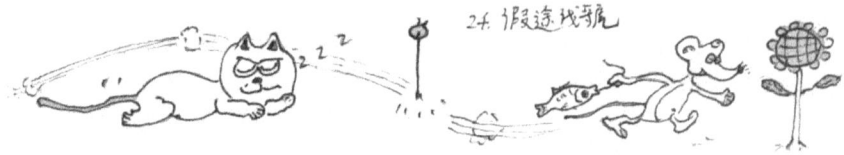

Sun Tzu said: When two of your enemies are in conflict with each other, intervene on behalf of one of them. Alternatively when two other countries are at peace with one another, bribe or coerce one to help you conquer the other. At the very least get a promise that they will not intervene when you attack the third party. This will give you influence over both.

When a small country is under threats from a superior enemy, a third party often places a posture of sending troops to infiltrate it. Of course, for a small country in the cracks, only sweet words will not gain its trust. One party often uses the name of "protection". Move quickly to control its situation and make it lose its autonomy, then take the opportunity to attack suddenly, and you can easily win.

Flower-dappled Horse and Turquoise Jade

During the Spring and Autumn period, the Jin state wanted to capture two small neighboring states: Yu and Guo. However, the relationship between the two small states was good. If Jin attacked one of them, the other one would send troops to rescue. Xun Xi, the prime minister of Jin, presented Duke Xian of Jin with a plan.

He said: In order to capture the two states, we need to alienate them so that they're unable to support each other. I heard that Duke Yu is quite greedy, we can just do what he likes. So I suggest that, your majesty take out two beloved treasures, the flower-dappled horse and turquoise jade, and give them out to him.

However, Duke Xian was unwilling to give out his treasures. Xun smiled and said: Don't worry, your majesty. Just let him take care of the treasures temporarily. Once his state is destroyed, everything will return to your hands.

Duke Xian accepted Xun's proposal and gave the treasures out to Duke Yu. Upon receiving the flower-dappled horse and turquoise jade, Duke Yu was overjoyed being dazed by the sudden offer.

Jin deliberately caused trouble on the border between Jin and Guo and made an excuse to attack Guo. Jin asked Yu to let the Jin army go through his state. Being offered benefits from Jin previously, Yu had to agree.

Duke Yu's minister, Gong Ziqi persuaded him not to do so. He said: The two states Yu and Guo depend on each other like humans' lips and teeth. Once Guo is dead, the lips are gone, and the teeth will turn cold. At that time, Jin won't let us go. Duke Yu simply replied that it would be a fool to make a weak friend while offending a strong friend.

The Jin army attacked Guo through the roads of Yu and soon won. On the way home, Li Ke, general of Jin, generously picked a lot of properties robbed and offered them to Duke Yu who thanked a lot and accepted. Li then pretended to be ill, said that he could not bring his troops back to his country, and wanted to temporarily station his troops near the capital of Yu. Duke Yu nodded without any suspicions.

A few days later, Duke Xian led a large army to visit here, and Duke Yu went out of the city to greet him. Duke Xian invited Yu to go hunting. After a while, Duke Yu suddenly saw a blaze in the capital from where thick tar-black smoke was belching and spiraling toward the sky. When he rushed back to the city, he found that the capital had been occupied by the Jin army. By this way, Jin easily destroyed the Yu state.

Safe Passages to Your Business

1) Safe passages and business operations

In today's business operations, there are many ways to "obtain safe passages". When competitors are experiencing tough times, you can use the "way" of joint operation and stock raising to control or merge their companies to satisfy your own intention. When your own power is weak, you can rely on other strong parties to seek bottom-up development; you can also expand your strength through technical assistance and financial support from other parties, or through other channels to proceed in a circuitous way and finally achieve victory over competitors taking up the market share.

2) Safe passages and market promotions

When conducting market promotions, your sales channels cannot be too single or narrow, a sales network is required to form by means of combinations of horizontal and vertical sales channels. In terms of advertising packaging and image publicity, you must also be deft at "obtaining safe passages" in promoting your products/services and arousing consumers' desire to buy.

Stratagem 25 · Replace Beams with Rotten Timbers

Sun Tzu said: Disrupt the status quo to throw your enemy off balance. Disrupt the enemy's formations, interfere with their methods of operation, change the rules which they stick to following, and go contrary to their standard training. In this way you remove the supporting pillar, the common link that makes a group of men an effective fighting force.

Forged Imperial Decree

After the Qin state had conquered all of the other warring states and unified all of China in 221 BC, Qin Shihuang proclaimed himself as the First Emperor, thinking that the whole country was unified and was the family business of his descendants for generations. He also believed himself was in good health, thereby none of his sons were named the heir to the throne.

In the palace, there were two powerful political groups. One was the eldest son Fusu and Meng Tian Group, and the other is the youngest son Huhai and Zhao Gao Group. Fusu was decent, gentle, and had a high reputation throughout the country. Qin Shihuang originally intended to appoint Fusu as the successor, and in order to train him, he sent Fusu to guard the frontier where the famous general Meng Tian was stationed. The youngest son, Huhai, was spoiled for a long time, and under the instigation of the eunuch Zhao Gao, he could only eat, drink and have fun.

In 210 BC, Qin Shihuang made his fifth southern tour. When he arrived at a village Shaqiu, he suddenly became ill. He knew that his time was up, so he quickly summoned Zhao Gao and Li Si, chancellor of Qin, and asked them to convey a secret decree to Fusu. Several days later, Qin Shihuang died.

Zhao and Li, in fear of Fusu and Meng Tian Group, secretly changed the emperor's final edict, which named Fusu, the crown prince, the heir to the throne. In the falsified edict, Fusu was ordered to commit suicide whereas Huhai was named the new emperor. After Huhai was enthroned as Qin Ershi, he promoted Zhao to Prefect of the Gentlemen of the Palace, an official post whose duties included managing the daily activities in the imperial palace. Zhao, who was highly trusted by Huhai, instigated the emperor to exterminate his own siblings to consolidate power, and used the opportunity to eliminate his political opponents such as Meng Tian and Meng Yi. He also framed Li for treason and had Li and his entire family executed, after which he replaced Li as chancellor and monopolised the state power.

2008 Chinese Milk scandal

In today's world, merchants may develop a habit of replacing beams with rotten timbers, i.e. making shoddy goods to gain huge profits, resulting in different levels of losses to consumers, or even threatening their lives.

The 2008 Chinese milk scandal was a significant food safety incident in China. The scandal involved milk and infant formula along with other food materials and components being adulterated with melamine. The chemical was used to increase the nitrogen content of diluted milk, giving it the appearance of higher protein content so as to pass quality control testing. Of an estimated 300,000 victims, 6 babies died from kidney stones and other kidney damage and an estimated 54,000 babies were hospitalized.

But how did this happen? Some stated that the source of the problem was farmers caught between rising costs and a government cap on prices. The farmers, these critics asserted, added the melamine to boost the tested protein level of watered-down milk. Farmers, in turn, blamed the operators of the thousands of milk collection stations scattered across the country, which purchased raw milk with little regulatory oversight.

Stratagem 26 · Point at Mulberries While Cursing Locusts

Sun Tzu said: To discipline, control, or warn others whose status or position excludes them from direct confrontation; use analogy and innuendo. Without directly naming names, those accused cannot retaliate without revealing their complicity.

Ostensibly, this stratagem refers to pointing at A while cursing at B. But in fact, like some other stratagems such as "kill the chicken to scare the monkey", "knock the mountain and shake the tiger", its connotation is more profound. As an effective suggestive method, it is commonly used by combat commanders to deter subordinates and establish his leadership authority. In layman's terms, as a respectful military commander, his law is strict, the award and punishment must believe, and be keen on catching one or two prominent negative cases and dealing with them strictly so that all soldiers can take warning.

Knock the Mountain and Shake the Tiger

In 208 AD, Cao Cao led his army approached Jiangling attempting to attack Sun Quan. Cao said to Sun Quan: "I'm on the order of the emperor to crusade against rebels. Now that Liu Cong has surrendered and Liu Bei has also been defeated and fled, I lead 800,000 naval forces and prepare to battle against you. If you surrender to me, you can simply save your nation."

In such an emergency situation, Sun summoned the civil officials to discuss countermeasures. Some advocated surrendering to Cao while some were in favour of resisting the enemy. They started debating, and Sun had no idea for a while. At this time, Zhuge Liang came to Jiangdong on a mission to discuss the formation of an alliance between Liu and Sun (i.e. a Sun–Liu alliance) to counter Cao. Lu Su introduced Zhuge to the civil officials and scholars.

Zhuge was very witty and eloquent. Relying on his own three-inch tongue, Zhuge eventually silenced the civil officials and scholars who considered themselves to be superior. Impressed by Zhuge's talent, Sun stood up and said to everyone: "I and Cao, an old thief, are at odds with each other, and I swear to fight against Cao to the end." Then, he drew his saber and cut off a corner of the sand table, raising his voice: "From now on, whoever talks about surrendering to Cao will end up like this table!"

Seeing this scene, those who advocated surrendering to Cao were silent. Sun's practice of knocking the mountain and shaking the tiger forcibly suppressed different opinions and played a positive role in unifying internal thinking.

Dealing with Nitpickers

In today's competitive workplace, when an open office space format becomes popular, disruptive people surround us anywhere and everywhere. Sometimes it can take more efforts to deal with those who tend to "point at mulberries while cursing locusts" then dealing with bad bosses. They are highly critical and seem obsessed with finding mistakes. Nothing is good enough for them. Difficult coworkers can rub you the wrong way and force to act irrationally, which is not exactly a healthy situation in which you can succeed.

The good news is that, even though you can't change everyone else's behavior, you can always change your own. To help you survive in a tough environment you should learn how to handle nitpicker coworkers without hurting them.

— Make them feel like they're know it all coworkers (even if they aren't).

- Keep your own work-life balance.

- Respect them for persistence, detail-orientation but leave the place for time off.

- Don't feel guilty about taking care of yourself.

- Show collaboration rather than individual approach.

- Insecurity is often at the root of their criticism. Try to build them up sincerely by pointing out the good you see in them.

- Avoid being defensive. Defensiveness is oddly affirming to the constant critic.

Stratagem 27 · Feign Madness Without Becoming Insane

Sun Tzu said: Hide behind the mask of a fool, a drunk, or a madman to create confusion about your intentions and motivations. Lure your opponent into underestimating your ability until, overconfident, he drops his guard. Then you may attack.

Lost Life by Jealousy

During the Warring States Period, Pang Juan, general of the Wei State, being jealous of Sun Bin's talents, devised a scheme to exterminate Sun. He cut off Sun's kneecaps and imprisoned him in a pigpen. When Sun learned that Pang was going to put him to death, he had to resort to the ruse "feign madness" and suddenly went crazy. In order to verify whether Sun was really crazy, Pang Juan sent his cronies to monitor Sun.

When the cronies arrived the place where Sun resided, they surprisingly saw Sun dancing in a pigpen, scattering the food over the fence, and grabbing dung stuffed in his mouth, with a sound "yummy, delicious" yelled from his throat.

The cronies immediately reported to Pang what they had seen, Pang was convinced and relaxed his supervision of the poor man. Sun could go wandering in the market, but still seemed crazy. At first, Pang sent an entourage to supervise Sun from time to time. Later, he saw that Sun was insane all day, then had the guardian cancelled.

One day, an envoy of Qi visited Wei and after learning of Sun's grievance, he managed to bring him back to the Qi state. In 342 BC, the battle of Maling took place between Wei and Qi. Pang was lured to a narrow pass at night, where his army was ambushed by 10,000 archers led by Sun. The Wei army suffered a crushing defeat and the Wei crown prince was captured by Qi forces, while Pang committed suicide.

Asking for a Raise

Asking for a raise! It's probably one of the most nerve-racking conversations you've ever had — and unfortunately, you may need to repeat it many times over the course of your career. You need to have the knowledge to back up your claims and consider the mood and environment you're walking into. If necessary, you should pretend to be weak or even silly before you start to craft your pitch for the raise you deserve.

The atmosphere in the office seemed weird recently, and Irene had a hunch that something big would happen. Her company wasn't big, including the boss Justin and driver Peter, there were only a dozen employees. Most of them resided in dormitories that the company served, so the relationship between coworkers was relatively close. While chatting in private, they usually complained about the boss's ungenerosity and "evil" deeds, most of which were bare ridicule, and no one would actually take it to heart.

But the last few times were different. Coworkers had been chatting with some mysteriousness, no longer joking, and sometimes avoiding her. Irene faintly felt that what her coworkers were discussing must have something to do with Justin, and it should not be a trivial matter. As the boss's secretary, she should be closer to the boss. The matter discussed by coworkers must be of great importance, so they were scrupulous about her.

In fact, Irene was aggrieved. Although she was Justin's secretary, still she stood by the coworkers' side. Justin did not give her any extra benefits, how could she not be able to tell the "enemy and friend"?

Irene then met her best friend Grace who confided the truth. It turned out that coworkers thought the salary was too low, and they planned to meet Justin to negotiate a raise collectively. Because Irene was the closest person to Justin, Grace didn't tell her for fear that she would inform Justin in advance.

The company's wages were low, and colleagues often complained, but no one dared to mention this before Justin. In fact, Irene often felt sad about her meager salary, and she was pleased that colleagues could unite and fight this time. However, she knew Justin too well — He used to be a soldier who was impossible to be cowed into the compromise. Even so, Irene was able to perceive the potential deterrence of a unity on him.

Justin often asked Irene about the situation of her colleagues, as she was a close "confidant". In the past, Irene always lied to him, boasting how hard her colleagues worked and how greatly they admired the boss. However, sensing that her colleagues was about to "burst", Irene started to be "silly", often reporting to him "I saw Tina posted a resume online", "Jack's classmate wants to bring him to start a business together"......At the same time, Irene also became "talkative", usually when going out with Justin, she gossiped with Peter, reiterating her concern over the soaring prices of food and vegetables all the way.

A week had passed, and still the boss seemed to be quiet. Irene knew it was the time for her to toss the trump card.

"Colleagues now often hold private meetings and avoid me." said Irene to her boss unintentionally.

Justin pondered for a while and said: "Let's hold a company meeting by tomorrow. The main topic of the meeting could be — Wages will increase by 10% to hedge inflation."

When this was announced, everyone was surprised at first, and soon realized what'd happened and thanked Irene for her heartwarming ruse. Later Irene told Justin a secret: last time her colleagues avoided her to hold the private meeting just in order for the discussion of how to surprise her for her upcoming birthday.

Stratagem 28 · Lure Them onto the Roof, Then Take away the Ladder

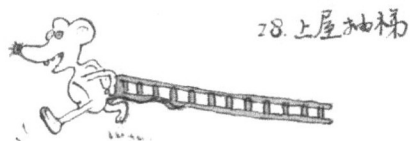 

Sun Tzu said: With baits and deceptions, lure the enemy into treacherous terrain and cut off their lines of communication and escape routes. To save themselves, they must fight both one's own forces and the elements of nature.

The key to this stratagem is to use profits to lure the other party. You must first set up a ladder, or show that there is a ladder that is convenient and safe for climbing up. Once he goes up to the roof, remove the ladder, making it impossible to advance or retreat but have to surrender.

Asking for Advice on Self-Preservation

In the late Han dynasty, Liu Biao, the warlord of Jingzhou, preferred his youngest son Liu Cong and wanted to designate him as his heir to the governorship of Jingzhou. Liu Qi, the eldest son of Liu Biao, being ostracized, feared that he would be framed by his brother, and turned to Zhuge Liang for advice on self-preservation. However, Zhuge refused to help him.

On one occasion, Liu Qi tricked Zhuge into climbing up a tower while visiting the garden. While they were chatting and feasting in the tower, Liu Qi secretly instructed his servants to remove the ladder.

He then told Zhuge, "Now, no way going up to Heaven nor going down to Earth. Whatever you say will be heard by me only. Can't you say something now?" Zhuge replied, "Sir, haven't you read that Shensheng was in danger because he remained in Jin whereas Chong'er was safe because he was outside Jin?" Liu Qi understood what Zhuge Liang was alluding to, and secretly came up with an idea.

Following the death of Huang Zu after the Battle of Jiangxia in 208, Liu Qi volunteered to be the new Administrator of Jiangxia, southeast to Jingzhou. Shortly after Liu Qi's move to Jiangxia Commandery, Liu Biao died suddenly and Liu Cong succeeded him as the Governor of Jingzhou. Liu Qi henceforth treated Liu Cong like an enemy, and might have attacked him had it not been for the arrival of Cao Cao's army.

In practical operations, every type of terrain can provide both an advantage for one form of warfare while a hindrance for another. A large force has the advantage in open terrain, while it is hindered by the narrow. But a small force is vulnerable in open spaces, yet protected by the narrow. Therefore, the key is to lure your enemy onto a terrain that hinders his abilities while helping your own.

Avoid Workplace Traps

In the workplace, beware of "being taken away the ladder while you are approaching the roof". A positive attitude and professional conduct can play a large part in a successful career. But if you're feeling down about your job and stalled on your career path, it could be because you've stepped into a workplace trap.

To avoid workplace traps, remain professional at all times, and don't take sides, or get sucked into arguments or recriminations. Help to make a workplace become more positive by not "fuelling the fire" and joining in negative politics. When a conflict arises, remember that there doesn't have to be a winner and a loser. It's often possible to find a solution that satisfies everyone.

If you're voicing concerns or criticism of your own, be confident and assertive but not aggressive. And make sure that you take an organizational perspective, and not simply a selfish one.

Avoid passing on rumors without taking time to carefully consider their source, credibility and impact. And don't rely on confidentiality. It's safer to assume that whatever you say will be repeated, so choose carefully what "secrets" you reveal.

As long as you're able to keep your distance, cover your own bases, have an honest conversation, and — of course — rise above, you'll be much more likely to handle that sticky situation with professionalism and politeness.

Stratagem 29 · Deck the Tree with Artificial Blossoms

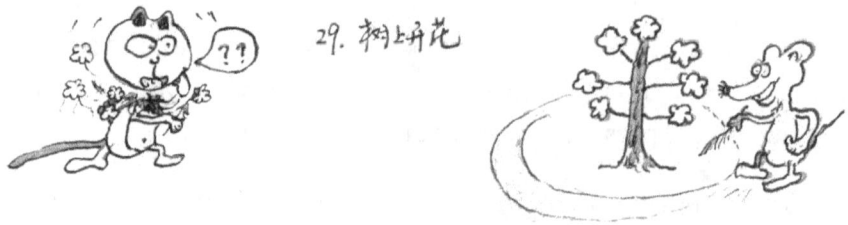

Sun Tzu said: Tying silk blossoms on a dead tree gives the illusion that the tree is healthy. Using artifice and disguise, make something worthless appear valuable and vice versa. Spreading out pennants and making the flags conspicuous are the means by which to cause doubt in the enemy. Analytically positioning the fences and screens is the means by which to bedazzle and make the enemy doubtful.

Decking the tree with artificial flowers means that there is no blossoms on the tree, but you can cut flowers with colored silk and stick them on the tree, making the forgeries look like real ones. If you don't look carefully, it's hard to tell whether it's true or false. This is commonly used in circumstances that your own strength is relatively weak, but you can utilize the power of friendly forces or some factors to create a false appearance of being strong.

Bellow of Rage

Zhang Fei, courtesy name Yide, was a military general serving under the warlord Liu Bei in the late Eastern Han dynasty and early Three Kingdoms period of China.

In 208, following Liu Biao's death, Cao Cao launched a military campaign aimed at wiping out opposing forces in Jing Province and the Jiangdong (or Wu) region. In the meantime, Liu Bei evacuated Xinye County and led his followers towards Xiakou, which was controlled by Liu Biao's elder son, Liu Qi.

Cao and his cavalry caught up to Liu's congregation at Changban, Dangyang, and Liu had to flee for his life, galloping south with Zhang Fei, Zhao Yun, and Zhuge Liang, while leaving his family and the populace behind.

Zhang commanded 20 horsemen as rearguard. He sent his troops into a nearby wooded area and had them move about frenetically as though their number was greater than it actually was. He then stood at the bridge; looking fierce and shaking his lance, he shouted: "I am Zhang Yide. Come and battle me to the death!" Such a bellow of rage instantly shocked Xiahou Jie, a general of Cao, to death.

Cao's soldiers also observed that the woods behind Zhang were clouded in dust and believed that there must be an ambush in the woods, so they retreated without a fight and Zhang destroyed the bridge and withdrew as well.

In fact, Zhang had earlier ordered his men to tie tree branches to the tails of their horses and ride around in the woods, churning up dust to create an illusion of an ambush.

Bird's Nest Olympic Stadium

The Bird's Nest Olympic Stadium, also known as the National Stadium, is a 91,000-capacity sports arena in Beijing. It was designed for use throughout the 2008 Summer Olympics and Paralympics and will be used again in the 2022 Winter Olympics and Paralympics.

In 2001, before Beijing was elected to host the Olympic Games, the city held a bidding process to select the best arena design which must meet the multiple requirements including the ability for post-Olympics use, a retractable roof, and low maintenance costs, etc.

In late November, Beijing turned wintery. Bidders from all over the world came to the city with great confidence in presenting their designs as they knew China wanted to have something new for this very important stadium — a collective building, a public vessel.

It was snowing, chilly and nippy. When Angel saw everyone stopping at the gate of the muddy, filthy construction site, she resolutely took off her shoes and trudged into the site through slushy roads. Upon seeing this, the engineers of the government panel were deeply touched. In the end, Angel's company was granted the contract to perform the stage lifting and lowering of the stadium roof as part of the construction process.

Of course, Angel didn't know the thirty-six stratagems at all. At that time, Angle just felt that she couldn't always wait at the front door and wanted to get in, so she strenuously walked in the site through the icy roads, whereas none of the other competitors did that. She just made a small action but gained the advantage in an evenly matched scene. This is the essence of "deck the tree with artificial blossoms".

Stratagem 30 · Turn from the Guest into the Host

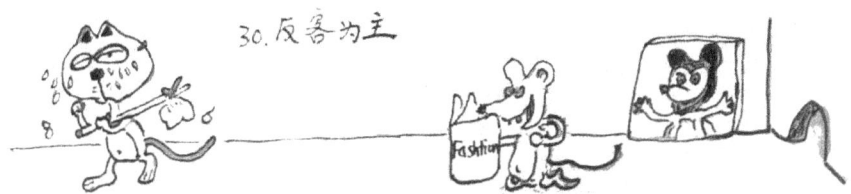

Sun Tzu said: Usurp leadership in a situation where one is normally subordinate. Infiltrate one's target. Initially, pretend to be a guest to be accepted, but develop from inside and become the owner later.

When you are weak but your enemy is strong there is no chance for victory in a direct contest. Instead, by assuming a subordinate position, you may have the chance of undermining and subverting your enemy's power.

Progressive Conspiracy

Literally, "turning from the guest into the host" is a process that exchanges the roles of host and guest via a "progressive conspiracy".

Xiang Liang (? - 208 BC) was a descendant of a family who served the Chu state in the Warring States period. His family lost power when Chu was defeated and annexed by Qin. In his youth he had killed a man and escaped with his nephew Xiang Yu to the Wu

100

state requesting asylum from Yin Tong, the governor of Kuaiji. Yin welcomed Xiang and appointed him an administrative position. During this time, Xiang made use of his fame and popularity to rally a group of supporters and secretly build up a militia.

In 209 BC, during the reign of Qin Ershi, peasant rebellions erupted throughout China to overthrow the Qin dynasty, plunging China into a state of anarchy. Yin wanted to start a rebellion as well, so he invited Xiang to meet him and discuss their plans.

Yin said: "All regions west of the Yangtze River are in revolt. The time has come when heaven will destroy the house of Qin. I have heard it said that 'He who takes the lead may rule others, but he who lags behind will be ruled by others.' I'd like to dispatch an army with you and your nephew at the head."

Xiang, who took the advice in a way the governor would regret, said, "This is a great honor you have bestowed on my family and I beg leave to call in my nephew Yu, so that he may receive your orders directly."

Yin consented. Xiang went to summon his nephew and secretly gave him instructions to hold his sword in readiness. They returned to the governor and after some time Xiang turned to his nephew and said: "You may proceed!"

This was the signal, and without hesitation Yu drew his sword and cut off the governor's head in a single stroke. Xiang then took the governor's seals of office and initiated the rebellion himself and rallied about 8,000 men to support him. Xiang proclaimed himself governor of Kuaiji and appointed Yu as a general.

Oracle of Omaha

Warren Buffett, the Oracle of Omaha, is one of the greatest investors of our time. His strategy for picking winning stocks starts with evaluating a company based on his value investing philosophy. Buffett looks for companies that provide a good return on equity over many years, and once invested, he would persist in long-term shareholding, slightly increasing his investment and gradually turning from the guest into the host — the most popular controlling shareholder of a company — step by step.

If one has to pick Buffett's single greatest investment of all time, there are several candidates: Coca-Cola, Apple, and Washington Post. All of these savvy investments have paid huge dividends for Buffett and Berkshire Hathaway over the years. However, out of all his top picks, Buffett's clear No. 1 investment is GEICO. "My favorite investment, one that embodies this philosophy, is GEICO, which I learned about when I was 20 years old," Buffett once told Forbes.

1) Wait For the Right Time

GEICO, which stands for the Government Employees Insurance Company, is now a wholly owned business of Berkshire Hathaway. But it wasn't always that way. In a stunning turn of events for such a competitively advantaged company, GEICO almost went bankrupt in 1976. By then, Davidson had retired, and the new executives running the company started to vastly underestimate GEICO's claims losses resulting from inflation. Losses soon grew, and by 1976, GEICO was on the edge of bankruptcy.

Fortunately, Jack Byrne joined the company as CEO in 1976 and took drastic remedial measures that fixed the mess. Berkshire bought a large amount of GEICO stock in the second half of 1976, and later increased its holdings slightly. By the end of 1980, a total of $45.7 million had been invested and Berkshire owned one-third of GEICO equity.

2) Persist in Long-Term Shareholding

With GEICO restored to its former glory and its low-cost advantage intact, GEICO continued both grow and buy back stock throughout the 1980s, which increased Berkshire's ownership stake to 50% of the company, without a need for Buffett to buy any more stock himself. At the end of 1995, Berkshire bought out the remaining 49% that it didn't already own for $2.3 billion and took control of the whole company.

Stratagem 31 · The Beauty Trap

Sun Tzu said: Send the enemy beautiful women to cause discord within his camp. This strategy can work on three levels. First, the ruler becomes so enamoured with the beauty that he neglects his duties and allows his vigilance to wane. Second, the group of men will begin to have issues if the desired women court another man, thus creating conflict and aggressive behavior. Third, other females at court, motivated by jealousy and envy, begin to plot subversions that further exacerbate the situation.

King of Yue's Revenge

Goujian (reigned 496–465 BC) was the king of the Kingdom of Yue near the end of the Spring and Autumn period. In 494 BC, Yue was defeated by the Kingdom of Wu in the battle of Kuaiji, and later Goujian was captured. Goujian took his wife to the Wu court to serve his opponent Fuchai, the king of Wu.

Goujian appeared to be very loyal towards Fuchai; he helped with his horses and swept the palace's grave. One time, Fuchai fell very sick. The doctor at that time said it was a weird sickness and it could only be diagnosed by knowing the taste of the poop, but no one wanted to try this. Goujian was the only one who offered to taste the poop. His hard work on Fuchai's behalf earned him the king's trust and favour.

But secretly, Goujian had been nursing his bitterness by sleeping on straw with a sword beside his head and by tasting gall each morning during this tough time. While planning his revenge, Goujian's minister Wen Zhong suggested training beautiful women and offering them to Fuchai as a tribute (knowing Fuchai could not resist beautiful women). His other minister, Fan Li, found Xi Shi and Zheng Dan, and gave them to Fuchai in 490 BC.

Xi Shi's beauty was said to be so delicate that while leaning over a balcony to look at the fish in the pond, the fish would be so dazzled that they forgot to swim and sank below the surface.

Bewitched by the beauty and kindness of Xi Shi and Zheng Dan, Fuchai forgot all about his state affairs and at their instigation, killed his best advisor, the great general Wu Zixu. Fuchai even built Guanwa Palace (Palace of Beautiful Women) in an imperial park on the slope of Lingyan Hill, about 15 kilometres west of Suzhou. The strength of Wu dwindled, and in 473 BC Goujian launched his strike and defeated the Wu army. King Fuchai lamented that he should have listened to Wu Zixu, and then committed suicide.

Beauty and Workplace Power

Everyone has a different view of "beauty". According to Wikipedia, "beauty" is the ascription of a property or characteristic to a person, object, animal, place or idea that provides a perceptual experience of pleasure or satisfaction. The experience of "beauty" often involves an interpretation of some entity as being in balance and harmony with nature, which may lead to feelings of attraction and emotional well-being, namely, beauty is in the eye of the beholder.

Beauty is manifested in various forms and types in different contexts. At today's competitive job fair, maintaining a positive attitude and creating a professional image can help job candidates develop an aura of confidence that's not possessed by the majority of the competition. Aside from the appearance, one's personalities such as sincerity, enthusiasm, self-confidence, generosity, forgiveness, etc. can all be counted.

In specificity, if you care about your looks too much, that can be a double-edged sword. It can create opportunities for women in their careers but it also creates traps, challenges, and stigmas. According to Quora, 43 percent of managers admitted to overlooking someone for a promotion or pay raise because of the way she dressed, and 20 percent used this as grounds for dismissal.

Stratagem 32 · The Empty Fort Ruse

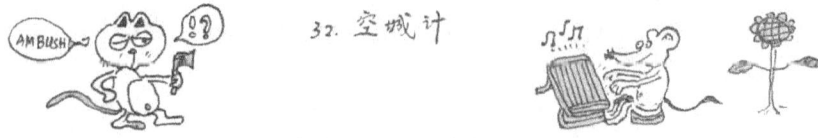

Sun Tzu said: When the enemy is superior in numbers and your situation is such that you expect to be overrun at any moment, then drop all pretense of military preparedness and act calmly so that the enemy will think you have hidden reserves. Unless the enemy has an accurate description of your situation, this unusual behavior will arouse suspicions. With luck he will be dissuaded from attacking.

Open City Gates

The novel "The Romance of the Three Kingdoms" described a wonderful story "Empty Fort Stratagem" in its ninety-fifth chapter. During the Three Kingdoms period, Zhuge Liang lured Meng Da to surrender and defect to his side, and let Meng ward off the Wei army in Shangyong, while he launched Northern Expeditions against Wei who, on the other hand, appointed Sima Yi to deal with the situation.

Knowing that his nemesis, Sima, just summoned out of the mountain at the time, then subdued Meng at lightning speed, Zhuge sent Ma Su to resist Wei at Jieting.

Having conspicuous talent in military theories though, Ma was literally a callow. He made a serious tactical blunder, resulting in a huge defeat and loss of Jieting. Sima took advantage of the victory and led 150,000 men to Xicheng where Zhuge's army was stationed. At that time, Zhuge had sent his troops out to collect grain so he had less than 2,500 men with him in the city, which was not well defended. Everyone was shocked when they heard the news that Sima's large army was coming.

After climbing up the viewing tower and looking afar for a while, Zhuge smiled and said to everyone: "Don't panic, I will let Sima retreat with a tiny scheme." He ordered all the gates to be opened, all the banners to be hidden, and soldiers to stay where they were. At each gate, 20 men disguised as civilians sweeping the streets. He put on a crane cloak himself and sat on the viewing platform above the west gate with two page boys flanking him. He then lit the incense, and then slowly played his piano.

When Sima arrived, he ordered the army to stop and spurred his horse towards the west gate. Not far from the west gate, Sima saw Zhuge sitting on the tower, with a feather on his back and a turban on his head. Gently fiddling and twiddling, he was leisurely playing the piano which sounded melodiously in the air. Two page boys stood behind, holding in hands a whisk and a sword. Alongside the gate, more than 20 civilians were sweeping, quietly as if no one was around.

Looked at that, Sima was surprised. Listened to the sound of the piano again, the high notes wailed like pelting rain, the low notes whispered in soft pain. Wailing and whispering, on a plate of jade pearls and beads were cascading fain.

While listening, a silver bottle suddenly burst, and strings resonated like cracked silk, wherein came the golden spears and armored steeds whining in dust.

Hurriedly Sima went back to his army and ordered a withdrawal. His second son, Sima Zhao, asked: "Isn't it because Zhuge has no soldiers in the city, so he deliberately composes an image like this? Daddy, why did you order the withdrawal?"

Sima looked at the sky and sighed: "Zhuge was cautious all his life and never took risks. Now, as I approach, he doesn't make any move, and the city gates are wide open, it must be either that he has something up his sleeve or that his reinforcements have arrived. If our army enters, it happens to be hit by his scheme. Moreover, there is a faint sound of golden spears and armored horses veiled in the melody of piano, so let's retreat quickly!" Hence he ordered the front to be the rear, the rear to be the front and retreated.

Reverse Psychology

Using the "empty fort" stratagem, Zhuge tactfully let the superior enemy retreat. This is an extraordinary story, but the psychology involved isn't so extraordinary, it's actually quite common in all walks of life. The successful execution of the empty fort stratagem, and more commonly reverse psychology, is at a specific time depending on the environmental factors.

Of course, such a strategy is based on deception and some may perceive deception as unethical. However you see it, look at your own experiences and assess the situations you've been in. In psychotherapy, doctors use paradoxical intention – the deliberate practice of a neurotic habit or thought to identify and remove a problem. In other words, you fix a problem by making it worse.

Note that reverse psychology is everywhere — If you resist something it usually persists. Try to be happy, and you'll always be sad. So if you can't sleep, you're advised not to sleep, and eventually you will sleep. Similarly, accepting fate, you often avoid fate; achieving more by actually doing less, or nothing at all.

Stratagem 33 · Counter-Espionage

Sun Tzu said: Let the enemy's own spy sow discord in the enemy camp. Undermine the enemy's ability to fight by secretly causing discord between them and their friends, allies, advisors, family, commanders, soldiers, and population. While they are preoccupied with settling internal disputes, their ability to attack or defend is compromised.

Fooled by a Fake Letter

This story happened during the Three Kingdoms period. Before the battle of red cliffs, Cao Cao led more than 200,000 troops and were stationed in Wulin on the north shore of the Yangtze River, intending to cross the Yangtze River to attack the Eastern Wu. Zhou Yu, the governor of the Eastern Wu, led his troops to confront Cao across the river, and the two parties were ready to fight.

Jiang Gan, courtesy name Ziyi, well-known for his talent at that time, served as an advisor for Cao. Because he had a close friendship with Zhou since childhood, he told Cao that he could voluntarily persuade Zhou to surrender without fight. Upon hearing this, Cao was overjoyed and set a wine to see Jiang off.

Cao's navy was composed mostly of northerners who were not used to living on ships. After Cao occupied Jingzhou, he appointed the defected generals Cai Mao and Zhang Yun as captains to train the navy in preparation for the conquering of the Eastern Wu. Cai and Zhang had lived in Jingzhou for a long time, and they're proficient in water warfare. The obvious enhancement of the naval might of Cao led by Cai and Zhang posed a potential threat to the Eastern Wu. Zhou was deeply worried.

On this day, when Zhou discussed matters with his subordinates, his old friend Jiang Gan came for a visit. Zhou knew Jiang's true purpose of the visit, so he tricked Jiang into believing that two of Cao's naval commanders (Cai and Zhang) were planning to assassinate their lord and defect to his side. Jiang also got hold of a letter apparently written by Cai and Zhang to Zhou, in which they claimed that they'd kill Cao soon and present his head to Zhou. He then stole the letter while Zhou was asleep, returned to Cao's camp, and showed him the letter. The letter was actually a fake letter written by Zhou. Cao fell for the ruse and ordered Cai and Zhang to be executed. He realised his folly later but it was too late already. Losing his two competent naval commanders, Cao consequently lost the battle of Red Cliffs later.

Jiang had originally wanted to persuade Zhou to surrender, he did not ever expect that his bosom friend Zhou was playing a counter-espionage ruse which caused Cao to kill his naval commanders, casting the shadow to the defeat of the battle of red cliffs later.

Leaked Recipe

The Coca-Cola company has a business creed: keeping your trade secrets means keeping your market shares. However, it also makes mistakes. In 2006, the company's "internal espionage" incident was revealed and described by major American media as more exciting than spy novels. In this case, Coca-Cola's executive administrative assistant Joya Williams attempted to sell a new product formula to its biggest competitor, PepsiCo, but that was reported by PepsiCo.

On May 19, 2006, PepsiCo provided Coca-Cola with a copy of a letter, the original of which was enclosed in a Coca-Cola's business envelope, and the recipient was PepsiCo. The sender claimed to be "Dirk" in the letter and was a "high-level staff member at Coca-Cola" who was able to provide PepsiCo with "specially detailed secret information". The Coca-Cola company promptly reported it to the FBI. After investigation, it turned out that the so-called "Dirk" was a man named Dimson from New York, who also had an accomplice, and it was determined that Joya was the source of the secret information.

The FBI immediately launched an entrapment operation. They sent an agent to pretend to be a PepsiCo connector and "purchased" a 14-page document from Dimson, which was later verified to be a genuine document of Coca-Cola. Dimson thought he made a big deal, and once again stated that he'd like to sell samples of the new product at $75,000, and the agent immediately instructed him to deliver the goods to the Atlanta Airport. Meanwhile, Coca-Cola's surveillance video showed that Joya had searched a lot of documents before she put some of them and a can of new beverage sample in her handbag. On July 5, the three persons were arrested when they were preparing to trade at the agreed place. In October 2006, Dimson and his colleagues pleaded guilty and were sentenced to 10 years in prison. In May 2007, Joya was sentenced to 8 years in prison.

Although the persons involved in the case were sentenced after the incident, the leakage of the formula has caused irreparable economic losses to Coca-Cola. This was not over yet. A man named

Mark Pendergrast later wrote a "biography" for Coca-Cola - "For God, Country, and Coca-Cola". The author published the formula of Coca-Cola in this book, and claimed that it was discovered by accident in an old file while studying the documents of Coca-Cola. There was a piece of paper marked with an "X" in the file with the names of all ingredients listed on it. Surprisingly, Mark immediately took pictures and copied them, and then managed to verify the authenticity of this recipe.

Coca-Cola officials firmly denied this, and repeatedly claimed that the Coca-Cola formula and its production process were still a secret. The Times reported that they successfully produced "Acton Coke" in a lab in Acton, west London, according to the formula published by Mark, and invited 10 experts to taste 6 kinds of soft drinks without labels such as "Acton Coke", "Coca-Cola", "Pepsi", etc. The results showed that their products were not much different from Coca-Cola in terms of color, smell and taste, which further proved that Mark's formula was credible.

Trade secrets are related to the survival of an enterprise. In today's highly competitive market, giving your own production, management, and sales information to others is tantamount to putting yourself in danger. The frequent occurrence of commercial espionage cases also reminds companies that they must raise their awareness of confidentiality in management and build up a security wall for themselves.

Stratagem 34 · Self-Torture Ruse

Sun Tzu said: Inflict injury on oneself to win the enemy's trust. Pretending to be injured has two possible applications. In the first, the enemy is lulled into relaxing his guard since he no longer considers you to be an immediate threat. The second is a way of ingratiating yourself to your enemy by pretending the injury was caused by a mutual enemy.

Zhou Yu Beat Huang Gai

Huang Gai, courtesy name Gongfu, was a military general who served under the warlord Sun Quan during the late Eastern Han dynasty of China. He previously served under Sun Quan's predecessors – Sun Jian (Sun Quan's father) and Sun Ce (Sun Quan's elder brother).

During the battle of Red Cliffs, Zhou Yu decided to dispatch a force at the head to confront Cao Cao. Huang courageously undertook the task. In the military meeting, Huang pretended to disagree with Zhou and even despised him in words, saying that he would surrender to Cao to keep the Eastern Wu safe. Zhou was furious and he ordered Huang to be executed, but with some intervention from other generals, he spared Huang's life and had him severely flogged. Huang then wrote a letter to Cao, expressing his willingness to defect over to Cao's side because he was unhappy with Zhou. Two spies planted by Cao in Zhou's camp, confirmed Huang's account and convinced Cao that Huang's defection was genuine, even though Cao initially saw through the ruse. Huang then arranged with Cao that on a certain night, he would sail across the river over to Cao's camp.

One night when the twilight fell, someone told Cao that Huang was leading his squadron over here to surrender. Cao led his subordinates and stood waiting at the bow. Sure enough, Cao was very proud to see Huang leading more than a dozen boats, sailing downwind.

As Huang's "defecting" squadron approached the midpoint of the river, the sailors applied fire to the ships before taking to small boats. It turned out that the ships had been converted into fire ships by filling them with bundles of kindling, dry reeds, and fatty oil. The unmanned fire ships, carried by the southeastern wind, sped towards Cao's fleet and set it ablaze.

Since Cao's warships were chained to each other, they could not escape, and immediately the whole fleet became a sea of flames, a large number of men and horses either burned to death or drowned. Cao hurriedly abandoned the ship and went ashore, but the barracks on the shore where the food was collected were also ambushed and burned by Wu's forces. Seeing the situation was hopeless, Cao then issued a general order of withdrawal and destroyed a number of his remaining ships before the retreat.

This stratagem has been evolved into a two-part allegorical saying later: Zhou Yu Beat Huang Gai – the punishment is appropriately given by one and willingly accepted by the other. It is used as a metaphor to mean something that both parties are willing to do.

Self-Torture: Buying a House

In modern business activities, operators may use the "self-torture" strategy to destroy their unqualified products intensively to attract the attention of consumers, establish a good image of their own business, and lay the groundwork for making more profit margins afterwards.

Here's an application of "self-torture" in business negotiations which has ever circulated on the Internet. Lucas had been looking to purchase a new home in his city. After several months of researching his purchase across the city, he found a house of his choice. At the initial look, he promptly told the seller's realtor that he agreed to make an offer on the property.

At night he called his friend Tim about his decision. Tim helped Lucas analyze the potential trade-offs based on current real estate market, but still thought the asking price of the chosen property was a little bit higher, he then suggested a scheme to probably trim down a few bucks.

When Lucas took Tim to look at the house again, Tim, pretended to be extremely discerning, or even picky. While touring the house, Tim started complaining about a lot of "issues": cracks in ceiling, rot/decay in doors and wood trims, peeling paint, damaged stucco, noisy exhaust fans. In front of the seller's realtor, Tim even reproached Lucas for preparing to sign an offer without careful inspection. Lucas pretended to be embarrassed, thus gaining sympathy from the seller's realtor who subsequently agreed to make some concessions on the purchase price if Lucas could sign the offer on that day.

In this case, Lucas and his friend Tim were obviously playing two roles: Huang Gai and Zhou Yu, respectively. It can be seen from the case that for the "self-torture" ruse to succeed, two conditions must be met: first, the roles of "Zhou Yu" and "Huang Gai" must be true enough that it will not arouse any suspicion from other parties; second, use other's empathy to let them make concessions.

Stratagem 35 · Chain Ruse

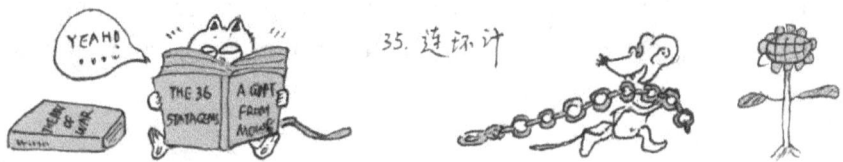

Sun Tzu said: In important matters, one should use several stratagems applied simultaneously, or one after another as in a chain of stratagems. Keep different plans operating in an overall scheme; however, in this manner if any one strategy fails, then the chain breaks and the whole scheme fails. When you set up ploys and opponents fall for them, then you win by letting them act on your ruse. As for those who do not fall for a ploy, when you see they won't fall into one trap, you have another set. Then even if opponents haven't fallen for your original ploy, in effect they actually have.

Chain Fleet Together, Seal Their Fate

Pang Tong (179–214), courtesy name Shiyuan, was an adviser to the warlord Liu Bei in the late Eastern Han dynasty of China. Pang appears as a character in the 14th-century historical novel Romance of the Three Kingdoms, which romanticizes the historical events before and during the Three Kingdoms period. In the novel, Pang Tong is portrayed as a brilliant military strategist who equals Zhuge Liang. Sima Hui recommended Pang and Zhuge as talents to aid Liu Bei by saying, "Hidden Dragon and Young

Phoenix. If you can get either of them, you'll be able to pacify the empire."

Before the Battle of Red Cliffs, Jiang Gan recommended Pang Tong to Cao Cao. Pang presented a "chain links strategy" to Cao. The plan involved linking Cao's battleships together with strong iron chains to make the ships more stable when they were sailing, as well as to reduce the chances of Cao's soldiers falling seasick due to excessive rocking. This led to Cao's defeat as his battleships were unable to separate from each other during the fire attack launched by the Wu-Shu alliance, and when one ship was set aflame, the other ships linked to it caught fire as well.

The allied victory at Red Cliffs ensured the survival of Liu Bei and Sun Quan, giving them control of the Yangtze and provided a line of defense that was the basis for the later creation of the two southern states of Shu Han and Eastern Wu.

The battle of Red Cliffs passed down many literary quotations involving the following ruses:

- Stir up the Water to Catch Fish (Zhuge Liang: Borrow Arrows With Thatched Boats)

- Counter-Espionage (Jiang Gan: Fooled by a Fake Letter)

- Chain Ruse (Pang Tong: Chain Fleet Together and Seal Their Fate)

- Self-Torture Ruse (Zhou Yu Beat Huang Gai)

- Praying for the Wind (Zhuge Liang: Pray for the Eastern Wind)

Systemic Approaches to Management

The use of chain stratagem involves various ruses forming an overall scheme. If any one ruse fails, then the chain breaks and the whole scheme fails. Therefore, controlling the overall situation from a systemic level is the key to the implementation of this strategy.

In today's business world, when things get complicated in organizations, people can be tempted to "break them up" to try and simplify. Divide and conquer. That just makes matters worse because organizations are in fact whole systems. Everything inside is interconnected and interdependent, so when people try and manage organizations any differently they inevitably underperform.

Therefore, managers today should think systemically and understand how to improve continuously the entire system that they govern. This does not have to be an innate talent. People can learn to develop systemic understanding through the right methods and tools.

In essence, systemic approaches to management must focus on certain aspects such as effectiveness, problem solving, responsiveness, flexibility, adaptability, creativity, and innovation. Such an organization carrying out the systemic approaches is able to respond in a timely manner to environmental change because employees are empowered to be creative, to experiment, and to suggest new ideas. The process of innovation is triggered by employees throughout the organization in a "bottom-up" manner.

Stratagem 36 · Retreat If All Else Fails

Sun Tzu said: Run away to fight another day. When your side is losing, there are only three choices remaining: surrender, compromise, or escape. Surrender is complete defeat, compromise is half defeat, but escape is not defeat. As long as you are not defeated, you still have a chance. This is the most famous of the stratagems, immortalized in the form of a Chinese idiom: "Of the Thirty-Six Stratagems, fleeing is best."

Retreat in Order to Advance

In order to expand his power, Duke Zhuang of Chu sent troops to attack Yong — a small vassal state. Since the Yong army struggled to resist, it was hard for the Chu army to advance. Yong also captured Chu's Lieutenant Yang Chuang in a battle. But due to Yong's negligence, three days later, Yang escaped.

"Soldiers of Yong are fighting hard. If we don't mobilize our main forces, it may be difficult to win." said Yang to Shi Shu, General of Chu, after reporting the situation of Yong.

Shi pondered for a while and came up with a scheme. He ordered an attack but soon after the battle began, the Chu army seemed unable to parry and retreated. Over the next few days, in the same way, the Chu army retreated in defeat again and again. When the Yong forces continuously won the seventh time, they had gradually become boastful and arrogant, showing no respect for their enemy. Within months, the Yong army's mind was paralyzed, its fighting spirit gradually declined, and its guard constantly slackened.

Shi then told his men: "Our army has pretended to be defeated seven times, the enemy now seems to be rather boastful whereas its morale is actually depleted. Let's stage a general offensive right now!"

Shi ordered his troops to strike at the capital of Yong. Reveling in victories, the soldiers of Yong never thought that the Chu army would suddenly return, they rushed to defend but were soon defeated. In the end, Chu conquered and annexed Yong in one fell swoop.

Business Exit Strategy

Within a global context of increasing competition, it is sometimes appropriate to exit markets you have entered with high expectations. Market exit constitutes a major business strategy decision, reflecting a strategic initiative on the part of a company to reshape its product/market positioning. Such exit occurs largely in response to a sustained loss-making situation or poor profit rate or low perceived growth potential.

An effective exit strategy should be planned for every positive and negative contingency regardless of the type of investment, trade, or business venture. This planning should be an integral part of determining the risk associated with the investment, trade, or business venture.

A business exit strategy is an entrepreneur's strategic plan to sell their ownership in a company to investors or another company.

An exit strategy gives a business owner a way to reduce or liquidate their stake in a business. If the business is successful, make a substantial profit; otherwise an exit strategy (plan) enables the entrepreneur to limit losses.

An exit strategy may also be used by an investor such as a venture capitalist to prepare for a cash-out of an investment. For traders and investors, exit strategies and other money management techniques can greatly enhance their trading by eliminating emotion and reducing risk. Before entering a trade, an investor is advised to set a point at which he will sell for a loss and a point at which he will sell for a gain.